CONVENT OF THE SACRED HEART

WOLDINGHAM

Prize for   Christian

Doctrine

Awarded to:-

Nicola Wheatley

BERNADETTE AND THE BEAUTIFUL LADY

BERNADETTE OF LOURDES

Shepherdess, Sister and Saint

by

FRANCES PARKINSON KEYES

LONDON

HOLLIS & CARTER

First published 1941 under the title THE SUBLIME SHEPHERDESS
Reissued in a revised and enlarged edition 1953
Reprinted 1955.

Nihil obstat
    John M. A. Fearns, S.T.D.
                  CENSOR LIBRORUM.
Imprimatur
    ✠ Francis Cardinal Spellman,
           ARCHBISHOP of New York.
New York, January 12, 1953.

MADE AND PRINTED IN GREAT BRITAIN PHOTOLITH-MECHANA LTD., LONDON, E.C.1
FOR HOLLIS & CARTER LTD., 25 ASHLEY PLACE, LONDON, S.W.1

AGAIN

TO ELEANOR CARROLL

WHOSE CONFIDENCE GAVE ME

STRENGTH AND COURAGE TO

WRITE THIS BOOK DURING

DESPERATE DAYS

THIS BOOK HAS BEEN READ AND APPROVED BY HIS
EXCELLENCY, PATRICE FLYNN, BISHOP OF NEVERS,
FATHER P. LEMAITRE, CHAPLAIN OF ST. GILDARD'S
AND EDITOR OF "REVUE BERNADETTE," AND THE
MOTHER GENERAL OF THE SISTERS OF CHARITY AND
CHRISTIAN INSTRUCTION OF NEVERS

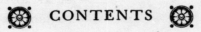

CONTENTS

ILLUSTRATIONS

BLESSED are the poor in spirit, for theirs is the kingdom of heaven.

BLESSED are the meek, for they shall possess the earth.

ST. MATTHEW V, 3 AND 4.

❀ FOREWORD ❀

I

IT IS MORE than fifteen years since I first tugged at the long iron bellpull hanging beside the grilled gateway of the Abbaye des Benedictines at Lisieux which, when it swung ajar, admitted me to a new heaven and a new earth. And even before I finished the biography I wrote that summer—the life of the lovely young saint now known as Thérèse of the Child Jesus, who, as Thérèse Martin, went to school in the ancient Abbaye—I was obsessed with the idea of writing a life of St. Bernadette—Marie Bernarde Soubirous—as a companion volume. This feeling grew stronger each of the many times I revisited Lisieux, and also each of the times, fewer in number but equally significant, that I visited Lourdes and Nevers. For it seemed to me, from the beginning, and it still seems to me, that the lives of these two complement and clarify each other.

There are many reasons why I should feel this way. The background and tradition of the two girls were entirely different: Thérèse was the cherished child of cultured and wealthy parents, the Benjamin of her father's advancing years, the darling and delight of four elder sisters. Bernadette was herself the eldest of a large family, the daughter of a poverty-stricken miller and a warm-hearted but improvident peasant. The greatest handicaps to serenity which Thérèse was obliged to meet were supersensitivity and excessive scruples, while Bernadette was compelled to combat poverty and ignorance before she could achieve even the elementals of decent livelihood and rudimentary learning. Thérèse was a grave and meditative Norman, whose mental and spiritual processes were orderly in the extreme, and whose "Little Way" was of far more significance in her own life and has become of more significance to her devotees than her isolated and infrequent supernatural experiences. Bernadette was a merry and industrious Bigourdane, whose visions transfigured her existence and created a cult which has since become universal. Thérèse so dominated her surroundings that multitudes who kneel before the flower-decked statues of the young Carmelite, or patiently and prayerfully await a "shower of roses" from her, only vaguely visualize Lisieux as a place. Bernadette, on the other hand, so submerged her identity in her apparitions that the pilgrim to Lourdes, seeing the grotto of glorious revelations, is aware primarily of this, and only incidentally of the lowly girl who was the instrument of such lofty grace. Indeed, the grotto is, and long has been, a universally familiar sight and one does not have to be a pilgrim or go to Lourdes to recognize it. Currier and Ives, who seldom depicted scenes connected with religion, much less Catholicity, made it the subject of one of their most interesting prints; and now there are reproductions

x

and representations of the shrine all over the world.*

These are the outstanding points of difference between the two, though there are many lesser ones; but divergent as their ways seem, they still retain many of the same attributes. In the first place, they are both saints of our own times. We do not have to grope far into the shadowed past to reach them. It was still possible, when I first went to Lisieux, Lourdes and Nevers, to talk, freely and frankly, with persons who knew them in the flesh and who could give our own impression of them substance and vitality. They seem real no less than close, and this, to the average woman who seeks to understand them, is of supreme importance. In the second place, there are, after all, many characteristics which they share. Their virtues are in no essential respect at variance. They were alike intelligent, composed and full of fortitude; hysteria and cowardice were alien to their nature and to their fine mentality. Their respective vocations were not foreign in form, and they brought honor not only to their religious calling but also to their country. Both were French-women—and France is fortunate in producing such daughters as these, who bear eternal witness to her integral spirituality. Their lives were alike illumined by faith; and in death, which came to both early, as a release from suffering long and bravely borne, they were beautiful and glorious. The world has acclaimed them impar-

---

* I know of three in Louisiana within a hundred-mile radius, each of which is distinctive, arresting and inspiring; the one in the church of St. Martinville, which was built by an untutored slave; the one in the church of St. Michael at Convent, which is made of bagasse; and the one which beatifies the grounds of the parochial school at New Iberia, and which is always illuminated in connection with the Christmas *crèche*.

tially, and this acclamation came, first of all, from the humble and the distraught, from the sick whose pain they had assuaged and the sad whose sorrow they had allayed.

It was with all this in mind that the idea of writing a biography of Bernadette, as well as the biography of Thérèse, entered my mind. At first it was nebulous. But it took firmer form with the kind and cordial reception accorded to *Written in Heaven: The Life on Earth of the Little Flower of Lisieux.** I resolved to return to France at the earliest possible moment for the purpose of gathering material for the story of the sublime shepherdess of Lourdes. But this moment, first for one reason and then for another, was again and again deferred. When at last I was free to go, I left home happily unaware that my personal opportunity would prove coincident with a world cataclysm.

After landing at Havre, Lisieux was again my first objective. It is very near the "Port of Grace," as the crow flies; and it is my own surest and safest harbor, my first manifest destination in the course of every journey. But I did not linger there that time. Lightheartedly, in my own comfortable car, and accompanied by Katharine McKiever, a fellow writer and "the good companion" of this particular adventure, I set out for Lourdes. Chartres had been chosen as our first stopping place. Katharine had never been there, and I looked forward with joy to guiding her into the cathedral at sunset, when the light streams through the jeweled glass, and shafts of radiance form pools of sapphire and emerald and ruby on the

---

* The title under which my biography of Thérèse first appeared. It has now been reissued under the title of *Thérèse: Saint of a Little Way.*

xii

stone pavement. As we saw the dissimilar towers from afar off, their spires of "frozen lace" rising above the great plain which they dominate, my gladness grew. But as we swung into place before the matchless façade, a sinister sight met our eyes.

In place of wide-flung doors, there were locked gates. In place of the glorious glass, there were gaping holes. The cathedral was closed. A guard told us that by order of the Beaux Arts, its chief treasures were undergoing removal to a secret place of safety.

In stunned silence we looked at each other. Those gaping holes, that closed cathedral, told us all too plainly that war had begun; despite the rumblings which had presaged it, the actuality came as a shock; and I am rather proud to think, after all these years, that it did not even occur to us that our safest course would be toward the nearest port where we could embark for home. I was at last in pursuit of a certain story which I had long wanted to write; and Kitty, though on leave from her news syndicate, realized that she had unexpectedly found herself in a situation about which it was imperative she should write full and immediate reports. Without hesitation, we took the long straight road which leads through the "granary of France."

It was after eight when we reached Orléans. The *patronne* herself emerged from our chosen hotel to help us with our luggage. Yes, she still had two rooms left, her last two. She did not know whether they would suit us, or the service, either. Half of her staff had been mobilized that afternoon. She was doing the best she could. If we would be pleased to enter—

We found ourselves engulfed by the military. All

around us were khaki-clad men. Some of them were elderly, many middle aged. Not a few wore the tarnished medals and bore the permanent marks of the war that was to make the world safe for democracy. Their wives and daughters were with them—plainly dressed women who did not speak much and who did not smile at all. They had seen all this happen before; they knew what it meant. At one table a graceful blond girl, wearing a pink blouse and a tweed skirt, was seated alone. She faced the door and her eyes never left it. A heavy-jowled, lumbering waitress brought in one dish after another and took it away again untouched. The girl did not even know that food had been set before her. At last a tall, slim officer clove his way through the crowd and caught her in his arms. An hour later, they were still sitting with interlaced fingers, drinking in each other's words, forgetful of the impending war, oblivious of the world.

We rose early the next morning and went to Mass at St. Paterne, the church across a small square from the hotel. As soon as Mass was over, we started for Nevers, following the Loire through its beautiful smiling valley, and stopping for lunch at the Hôtel du Rivage at Gien, famous for its food. The fame is well merited, and the food was served—with great willingness and considerable delay—to a large crowd by two overburdened but uncomplaining waitresses. Again we saw khaki all around us, and people were avidly reading the newspapers and talking about *les évenements*. The embankment at Gien is a tranquil place, especially at noontime, when everyone is indoors agreeably occupied with eating. But for once we did not find it completely deserted at this hour. Two men were busy with paste pots and placards, putting

xiv

up notices. The paper was limp but the text was stern, for these were notices of mobilization. When we reached Nevers, late that evening, the scene was much the same. It boasts a very proud hostelry, the Hôtel de France, where Napoleon stopped twice, as you may read by the stone tablets affixed to the wall on either side of the front door. But again, the *patronne* met us with a troubled face. Would we be willing to have a little indulgence? Because half the personnel—

We were awakened the next morning by strange sounds in the street. Normally, Nevers is a very still city, dormant and gray. But now it was astir. Men of all sorts and conditions were streaming through it. They wore civilian clothes, for the most part very shabby, and they carried small, cheap suitcases and paper packages, negligently tied up with string, in their hands. They were unshaven and unkempt, but for all that they retained the invincibly jaunty air of the average irrepressible Frenchman. A couple of hours later, as we went to keep our first appointment at the Motherhouse of the Sisters of Charity and Christian Instruction—where Bernadette was once a nun and where she now lies enshrined—our own progress was blocked by these same men as they poured out of a mobilization center. They were now wearing the peaked blue hat of the *poilu* and clumsy, ill-cut uniforms. They pulled down their blouses as they went along, and tilted their cigarettes between their teeth, and some of them laughed and sang snatches of songs. That is the way the *poilus* are. But all the time I was inside the convent— and it was a long time—Katharine sat outside in the car and the *poilus* never stopped streaming past. When I finally came back, she looked very serious. She was in

France with the Red Cross in that other war—the one that was to make the world safe for democracy. She had not forgotten how it was.

Of course a logical way to study the story of Bernadette is to go to Lourdes first, and afterward to Nevers, because it was at Lourdes that she lived for the first twenty-two years of her life, and only afterward that she went to Nevers. But you cannot always proceed logically if you are racing a war across a country in order to get your story. This same race prevented us from lingering long in Nevers. We went back and forth between the hotel and the Motherhouse so that I could keep the appointments and hold the conferences and see the sights that were indicated. Between conversations with the Superior and the Sisters, we also had one with that distinguished cleric and great gentleman, Patrice Flynn, Bishop of Nevers, whose coat of arms is emblazoned with a shamrock, which is his Irish heritage, but whose preferred speech is the flowing French of his adopted country. Like the nuns, he was helpful in every possible way and one of these ways was in expediting my work. Soon we had started on our way again.

Our route now took us through a land of constantly increasing loveliness, "the other château country," as it is sometimes called to distinguish it from the better-known château country of Touraine. It was Limousin, Périgord and Gascony that we were traversing now, verdant and sunny. Heather bloomed along the way, a panoply of feathery amethyst; fluffy clouds rose like plumes in the soft sky. The light was clear and dazzling. We saw hills crowned with castles, tawny in the mellow gloaming, and with churches whose substantial towers

Photograph by Elemore Morgan

CURRIER & IVES PRINT DEPICTING THE GROTTO AT LOURDES

Photograph by Elemore Morgan

SHRINE OF OUR LADY OF LOURDES (MADE
BY A SLAVE) AT ST. MARTINVILLE, LA.

rose foursquare to the heavens; around these clustered red-roofed houses, separated by slitlike, cobbled streets. Between the medieval towns, one gracious valley cupped between bright hills succeeded another. It was a land in which we could have lingered indefinitely, had we not been bent upon a special errand and harassed by haste. There had been no way of making advance reservations anywhere, for the telephone system was already closed except to official calls, and telegrams had to be submitted first to the mayoralty and afterward taken to the post office before they could be sent off—a process which we tried once and promptly abandoned, because it consumed too much valuable time. Our faithful car sprang a sudden leak, and we were left stranded on a hill for two hours before we could get help. When we finally reached a gasoline station, all the *essence* we could buy was the cheap and unreliable "tourisme"—the excellent American brand on which we depended being already conserved for the military; and we went to four garages without finding a single mechanic who could make the necessary repairs. There was nothing to do but push on, hoping that with a full tank we could beat the leak to the next large city.

We spent the night at Limoges, but did not delay for even an hour to look at the far-famed enamels manufactured there. We lunched at Bergerac, but left without stopping to see the sights symbolic of Cyrano. And finally we entered Lourdes at twilight, having come, in thirty hours, halfway across a country in the process of mobilization, and feeling, in a way, as if we were part and parcel of it, when one garrison town after another disgorged the occupants of its barracks across our path.

The first sight of the Pyrenees is breath taking; Lourdes, nestled serenely at the foot of these mighty mountains, is a mystic and hallowed city. We wound our way through its curving streets with a sense of strangeness intermingled with our sense of reverence. For these streets were empty. All pilgrimages had been canceled. There was no bustle among the shops, no sign of the sick or the devout, no fervent preparation for a torchlight procession. The Gave, flowing green and peaceful between its embankments, made the only sound we heard. As we drew up at the door of the hotel to which we had been commended, we saw that all its shutters were drawn. Again, as the *patronne* came out to meet us, it was with an apology. But this had a different quality from those we had heard before. There was reserve in it, a note of tragedy. Unlike the hotels we had been in previously, all filled to overflowing, this was empty except for ourselves. Its vacancy was even more uncanny than that of the streets, but we were too exhausted—and at the same time too exultant—for disquietude. We had run our race with the war. We were in Lourdes. Nothing could dislodge us now. We ate the excellent dinner silently served us in the deserted dining room and sank gratefully into our comfortable beds.

The next morning Katharine could not rise from hers. A touch of ptomaine had felled her. For two weeks I had been struggling with the handicap of a sprained ankle; I had resolved to rest and nurse this when once I had reached my destination. But something impelled me to start limping downstairs after all. At the foot of the stairway stood the *patronne,* her eyes glittering with unshed tears, her mouth set in a straight line to conceal its trembling.

xviii

"Germany has invaded Poland," she said in a hard voice. "This is the beginning of the end. My hotel has been requisitioned by the government for a military hospital. It must be stripped of all its furnishings and made ready for reoccupancy within five days. I shall be obliged to ask you to leave at once."

"But we can't!" I cried. "We've only just come! We're not sight-seers, not pilgrims; we're writers! We've driven headlong across France to get here. I'm going to write a life of Bernadette. I've dreamed for years of doing it. I'd be willing to take any kind of risk rather than give it up."

"I am very sorry," the *patronne* said. But her lips were still set in a hard line as she said it. "Since your friend is sick, you may stay here one more night. But that is all. I do not know whether you can get accommodations elsewhere or not. Many hotels have closed for the season already, now that pilgrims are not permitted to come here any more. Others, like ours, will doubtless be requisitioned. I will try to get you a taxi. Most of the chauffeurs have been mobilized, but I will try. You can go out and see all that is possible in a day."

All that is possible in a day! Sights can be seen quickly enough, as a rule, if they are observed superficially. Documents can be read almost anywhere; facts can be gleaned after a fashion. But knowledge, the kind of knowledge which makes possible the writing based upon it, understanding, the illumination of the spirit as well as of the mind—how is it conceivable that these can be acquired in a day? To the best of my belief it has never been done by anybody; certainly it has never been done by me. But when a veteran of the war that was to make the world safe for democracy—still too disabled to fight again—was finally found to drive me around, I went feverishly from place to place, fighting overwhelming fatigue, fighting to disregard the increasing pain which every footstep gave me, fighting to keep tears of disappointment and bafflement from overflowing: to the Soubirous mill, to *Le Cachot,* to Bartrès, around the Lake of Lourdes and to several adjacent villages. As we went along, my chauffeur spread the tidings that had filtered in that day: Poland was indeed invaded; general mobilization had begun in France. A dark woman, with a quivering face and a blue shawl draped over her head and fastened under her chin, left her sheep grazing in their peaceful pasture and rushed down a hillside to the road. When she caught up with us, she entered into prolonged conversation. So did several other persons who were no less picturesque, though equally piteous. It was late when we finally got back to town, and I was unresponsive to my chauffeur's suggestion that we should go to the Hospital of St. Bernadette. I urged him on.

"No, no, it is to the orphanage that I want to go," I insisted. "I have a letter to deliver to the Superior from her sister who is at the Motherhouse in Nevers. And there is a nun at the orphanage who knew Bernadette. I must talk with her before it gets too late."

Quite unmoved, my chauffeur swung stubbornly up the small hill leading to the hospital and drove up the driveway with a flourish. "This is where you should go," he reiterated. "This is where St. Bernadette herself lived for six years. It was not a hospital then, it was a school kept by the good Sisters of the same Order as those you saw in Nevers, and who are still here. Later on I will take you to the orphanage. But you must come to the hospital first. See, the Reverend Mother is already standing in the doorway waiting to receive you."

It was true. In the welcome shadow of the arcade, where bright flowers bloomed between tall stone columns, stood a woman of majestic mien, whose face, somber in repose, kindled when she smiled. She showed me the old and new chapels and the historic parlor. Then she led me to the rear of the building so that I might have a glimpse of the garden and the schoolrooms which now serve as wards. Wishing to make a little offering as a token of my appreciation, I fumbled in my purse, where I had nothing but one large note and a number of small coins; and failing to find anything appropriate, I asked her if she could change a thousand francs

"No, not easily, at the moment," she answered. "But please do not be concerned, madame. I have been only too glad to show you our souvenirs of Bernadette. You seem genuinely interested. Are you planning to remain long in Lourdes?"

"I meant to. I came here on purpose to write a life of your little Saint. But now I don't know how I am going to manage—"

Suddenly I was telling her everything—all that I had planned, all that I had hoped, all that had delayed and hampered me. She listened attentively, but so quietly that I myself was calmed. And when I paused for breath, she spoke reassuringly.

"*Voyons*," she said. "There is always a way to manage. You must not be so discouraged. Surely you have not persevered all this time in your idea of writing a book, and come a long distance under great difficulties, to give up at the last moment! Do you see that small building on the other side of the garden? It is a private clinic connected with our hospital. Your ankle is in bad condition, I can see that for myself, and you say the friend who is with you has had a touch of ptomaine. She would be better off if she had simple dietary food for a few days, just as you would be better off for a complete rest and quiet. I think Sister Stephanie, who is in charge of the clinic, could make you both very comfortable. Indeed, it is possible that she might be able to give you two connecting rooms, which I believe are vacant just now, and which lead out on a small terrace of their own. You could write there and have your meals there. It would be peaceful and pleasant. And later on, as soon as you are better, of course you can go out as often as you like. Come, we will go together and talk to Sister Stephanie about it."

So history repeated itself, as it has such a strange way of doing. For the second time I found my warmest welcome, not at an inn but at a convent—and not only a welcome but understanding and touching confidence coupled with compassion. A terrace had long been unalienably associated in my mind with my brief but beatific sojourn in the Holy Land. It is there the custom to repair to the housetops for meditation and repose in the cool of the evening; the experience of doing so is an unforgettable one. Here the revelation was different, but no less remarkable. Shielded from the dazzling sunshine, and still warmed by it, I sat in my big easy chair before my small white table—writing and writing and writing. On one side of me rose the verdant hills. There were grape arbors and palms and fig trees at the foot of them, and
xxii

as I looked at these, the biblical significance of the spot became intensified. Had I not myself found a "tower and a vineyard"?

On the other side of me stretched the convent garden. Roses clambered up on trellises to meet the overhanging branches of the chestnut trees, and dahlias big and bright as chrysanthemums formed a brilliant hedge, and spikes of gladioli pushed up through the rich soil which nourishes fruits and vegetables as well as flowers. Beyond was the charity hospital. I could see the old men and women coming out from their rooms to sun themselves on the long galleries. I could see the strong Basque serving maids airing the bedding in the sunshine and shaking the water from the lettuce I was to have for lunch. I could see the Sisters themselves going quietly about their appointed tasks. Sometimes they came to visit me. Sister Baptistine, the *Soeur Cuisinière,* was solicitous about the food she served me, though there was no reason why she should have been, for it was all delicious; but we conferred at length about salads and sauces. Sister Stephanie, the *Soeur Infirmière,* came to look at my foot, to assure herself of its improvement, and afterward lingered to talk about the war. She warned us that an order had gone forth that all lights must be out at nine o'clock, because of possible air raids, and explained other regulations to us. We listened to them attentively and obeyed them scrupulously. For we knew that at any moment there might be gruesome necessity for obedience. We had won our race with the war by getting to Lourdes before hostilities spread. But we could not win it in getting home, also. We did not know when or how we could do that. In fact, we knew very little about what was going on in the outside world. Censorship was very severe, and as the number of inspectors was still insufficient, many letters were purposely held up, unopened, on the theory that contraband news would lessen in value the longer it was delayed. We heard nothing from the United States at all. Not even during the autumn that I spent in Tierra del Fuego and Patagonia did I feel so completely shut off. For then cables came through anyhow, and one of my sons was with me. I would have given a good deal to see one of them—or even to hear from one—in Lourdes.

But it is surprising how much calmness can be developed under such circumstances. The only really bad moments came when the trains passed through. A narrow-gauge railway wound around the base of the mountain, and every hour or so a little toy train whistled and clattered past. At least it looked like a toy train at first glance, the engines were so absurd and the cars so tiny. But all these cars were crowded, some with horses, some with boys. They were packed close together, in freight cars, in carriages of all classes. The boys looked even jauntier than they had at Nevers. They were singing and cheering, and as they went by they waved their pointed caps and called out gay greetings to Sister Stephanie and to me. For Sister Stephanie seemed to know by instinct when the trains were coming and she went out into the garden and watched them with lingering eyes. I saw her from my terrace and, though her back was turned to me, I knew what the expression on her face was like. It was still stamped there when she came up a little later to see me. "Those poor youngsters starting off to their death!" she would say without any preamble. Her voice quivered, but she controlled it quickly. "Is your bandage comfortable?" she would inquire. "Do you think you would be better off in a different kind of shoe?"

Aside from the Sisters' occasional visits, for the most part I was alone. Katharine was well again; she was here and there about the town, seeing sights, making excursions, gathering news. Almost the only visit I made myself was to Madame Pierre Bertrand Soubirous—the widow of Bernadette's youngest brother—who was then still living and who, like the Superiors of the convent and the orphanage and several Sisters in both institutions, gave me invaluable help. I was thankful for the seclusion my terrace afforded. Gratefully, in this retreat I found the understanding and the knowledge for which I had sought so vainly that first day in Lourdes, and the illumination of the spirit as well as of the mind. The persons who had either known Bernadette in the flesh, or who had spent years in association with persons who did, made her seem very real to me and I was able to work fast. Before every kind of communication with the outside world was completely shut off and we were told that all gasoline was about to be commandeered, the framework of the biography was on paper. I knew that it would not suffer in any essential if I left Lourdes.

So Kitty and I motored to Bordeaux, the nearest port, and I went on working during the weeks while we waited for some sort of transportation across the Atlantic. This was finally found on a French freighter, and the writing continued while traversing mined waters, in such danger of submarine disaster that we were ordered to keep life preservers and small, ready-packed bags constantly within reach. Kitty remained calm and, like me, went on writing; but we were surrounded by a group of passengers in various stages of hysteria and terror, who had nothing to do but give vent to their fears. Providentially, I was busy every minute with the still uncompleted research and revision which I was pledged to finish within a given time; and the character of the work was so tranquilizing and uplifting that I was able to forget, for hours on end, the perilous conditions under which it was advancing. A new confidence was born in me that, having accomplished this much, I should henceforth "never fail through fear" to achieve anything which I undertook to do. I have not once lost this confidence in all the years that have followed.

II

On the whole, they have been happy and rewarding years, and they have been unblighted by great griefs and unthreatened by danger; but they have been so crowded that they have brought with them almost unrelieved tension, and they have been complicated by long periods of either partial or complete physical disability. All the travel undertaken in the course of them has been done under difficulties; it has been necessary to limit it to such expeditions as were almost inescapably indicated, in connection with my work; and it was not until this last summer that such expeditions took me anywhere near either Lourdes or Nevers. Then suddenly the way opened to visit both again.

My approach this time was from Spain, where I had been spending nearly two months with my two eldest grandchildren, Peter and Margaretta, and my secretary, Deanie Bullock. Peter had never visited a shrine before; Margaretta had been briefly to Montserrat in the course of a day's outing, but had never stayed in a city dominated by a shrine; and Deanie, though acquainted with some shrines less universally acclaimed than Lourdes, had not been to one so beatified with healing powers and so permeated with mystic meaning. I was very hopeful that they might all see this one as I had first seen it, many years ago, with my son John: on a still misty evening when the only supplicants at the grotto were so deeply devout, so desperate in their need and so unquestioning in their faith that even the most casual beholder immediately felt the force of their devotion, their necessity and their belief and presently came to share these. I have always remembered this sight and this experience as among the most moving in my life; I wanted my charges and my co-worker to carry away a similar memory.

But their first impressions of Lourdes—and I am afraid their lasting impressions—were very different. We had come a long way, we were all tired and we circled around and around, in a tangle of traffic, through streets lined with souvenir shops, whose wares were gaudy rather than godly, before we finally found our hotel. By a curious chance, this—I had forgotten its name—proved to be the same from which Katharine McKiever and I had been so peremptorily evicted in 1939 to make way for the military. Happily, there was no question of eviction this time. But there was the lukewarm, not to say grudging, reception which we found all too general on the Continent in places where the demand exceeds the supply.* Yes, it was true that such and such accommodations had been promised for such and such a date; but previous visitors had not left as soon as expected and only one room was ready so far; of course later on an adjustment could be made. When all four of us had crowded into the one room, we found that our interpretation of the word "ready" was not quite the same as that of the management. There were no pillow slips and no towels in evidence, and evidences of any recent cleaning were also lamentably lacking. Hoping to cheer my depressed companions, I suggested that we should go down to supper; by the time that was over I was sure—or so I said—that everything would be satisfactorily arranged. Alas! hungry hordes had preceded us and the presentation of the menu was only an empty gesture. The maître d'hôtel withdrew it almost as quickly as he had displayed it. He could, however, give us some cold ham. . . .†

Ham happens to be one of Margaretta's chief detestations and we were shivering with cold already, though this was July. (It seems always to be my fate, no matter where I go—except in Spain—to arrive there immediately *after* a period which, according to all reports, has been unprecedented for warmth and dryness!) Following a meager meal, we went back to our dismal rooms, as there was nothing else to do; the customary torchlight

* It was not so, as I have previously noted, at the outbreak of the war. At that time, when any lack of accommodations and service would have been understandable and excusable, the *hôteliers* did their level best, under trying circumstances, and honestly regretted that they could not do better. There has been a great change, which is not an improvement, in their attitude.

† It is perhaps permissible to note in passing that when the bill came in, there was a charge for the dinner—with ham as a supplement.

procession had been canceled because of the rain. Our quarters had been slightly expanded, but otherwise rendered no more attractive and, again speaking with forced cheerfulness, I said I thought everything would look much brighter in the morning.

Once more I was doomed to disappointment. The next morning the weather was still cold and cloudy, and as we entered the broad paved avenue which leads to the grotto we were startled by the shouts of an unkempt guard, who rushed toward us with loud imprecations, brandishing a cane. He wore a dirty cap as well as a soiled shirt and bedraggled uniform, and he was clutching the stub of a cigarette in his free hand, which was as begrimed as the rest of his person and his attire. It was not until we had recovered from the first shock of his threatening salutation that we gradually grasped its meaning: he was telling us that women and girls could proceed no farther with uncovered heads!

I was already wearing a hat, and Margaretta and Deanie both had scarves in their handbags, so the situation was quickly remedied as far as our own group was concerned. Directly behind us, however, were two ladies who were not so well provided, who understood no French and who were really alarmed by the raised stick and raucous voice. I tried to explain to them, but they could not be reassured. They had not intended to go inside the basilica, they told me, or to attend a service at the grotto; they were only walking along the avenue to get a general impression of their surroundings. Surely there was no regulation which required them to cover their heads out of doors, except at an outdoor Mass! Or, if they really had erred, was not the guard also in error? The same regulation which requires a woman to cover her head requires a man to uncover his! And as for the cane and the cigarette! . . . Why did the authorities not station a courteous attendant, with some qualifications as a linguist, at the entrance to the avenue—one who could and would explain the regulations and help visitors to comply with them, something after the manner that a similar service is performed at the Vatican? I could give no satisfactory answer to this question, because the same one had arisen in my own mind. The two ladies turned away and I am afraid they never went back. My own companions, of course, went on with me to the grotto. But first impressions are hard to erase, especially if subsequent ones are no more favorable; and bad weather continued to make processions impossible, while no other striking spectacles occurred. To the bewildered children, their first shrine was not a place of mystic beauty, but a place where they had been threatened with a stick. Deanie was strongly tempted to turn away, as the two ladies had done, and leave the grounds without even visiting the grotto. Though she did not do so, she went on to the shrine in a somewhat disillusioned frame of mind; and when we reached the grotto, this disillusionment became active resentment as her eyes fell upon a girl, strolling casually about, dressed in slacks!

I would not feel it was fair to tell this story if I believed our experience to represent an isolated case; but unfortunately I do not. Twice I returned to the avenue and each time I saw the same thing happen. After that, I spoke of it to several other persons and they had seen it, too. It would take far more than an episode of this kind, of course, to rob the zealous pilgrim of his fervor. But what

xxx

of the thousands who come to Lourdes hoping, if not actually for a miracle of healing, at least for a sublime revelation—and yet doubting whether these exist? Is it not too much to ask that they shall be receptive to the possibility of such wonders if they have first fought their way through hordes of hawkers, past unco-operative policemen, to some hostelry which is not a real resting place—and then been violently rebuked, in an unfamiliar tongue, to the accompaniment of a raised cane? And what of those others—less numerous, let us hope—but still not to be discounted, who are frankly incredulous and who come merely out of curiosity, or on a picnic jaunt or—worse still—seeking an occasion to jeer and to blaspheme? Is it not playing straight into their hands to receive them in such a way? Is the last slim chance of turning them from frivolity and disbelief and evil not dangerously jeopardized?

These were the disturbing questions to which, like the one that first arose, I found no satisfactory answer and which kept persisting throughout the day. But gradually I was able to dismiss them from my mind. Very naturally, the hospital was my first objective after the grotto. There I was greeted with sad tidings: my old friend, the Mother Superior, was sick unto death. Her assistant, who received me, could not conceal the grief which underlay her calm courtesy. Yes, of course, they all remembered me, and most kindly, she said. Sister Stephanie, who was still at the clinic, would be glad to see me. As for herself, she knew that I would excuse her. Their Reverend Mother had already been given Extreme Unction. . . .

Sorrowfully, I took my way through the garden to the clinic. And when I saw that the statue of Bernadette, as a child, with her lamb, was still in its accustomed place, surrounded by flowers, I began to feel at home again. A doctor, just emerging from the operating room, looked at me curiously; evidently not many outsiders find their way to its doors, even now. But when I explained my errand he was all cordiality, and a moment later Soeur Stephanie was greeting me with cries of joyous recognition and kissing me on both cheeks.

It was in her presence and through her talk of sickness and suffering of mind and body and of a healing power for both that I began to recapture the Lourdes I thought I had lost—and that I discovered can never be really lost, once you have found it. And later that same day, as I went over the rough road to Bartrès and came upon its sloping meadows, its rippling brook and its quiet sheepfold, the vision of the sublime shepherdess became clear again. I seemed to see her standing among her sheep, reciting her rosary while she watched over them. Again, as the bells in the village church rang for the Angelus, it seemed as if her gentle voice echoed their salutation.

"Hail, Mary, full of grace! the Lord is with thee; blessed art thou among women."

III

Our stay in Nevers did not begin much more auspiciously than our stay in Lourdes. We reached the former point at one o'clock in the morning, after a long hard ride, and though we had telephoned in advance to say we would be late, the rooms we had reserved had been given to someone else. The garage was already full, and there was only one overworked night watchman on duty. We

LOURDES

IN THE CLOISTER OF THE HOSPICE

dragged our most needed baggage to our limited quarters ourselves, and went hungry, thirsty and exhausted to bed.

This time, however, things really looked better to us in the morning. True, the bombed cathedral was a sad sight: much of its roof was gone, only fragments remained of its beautiful buttresses, its walls were rent with gaping holes and the figures on its damaged façade were mutilated. But all around it the workmen were busily sawing the soft stone, which is so readily adaptable to rapid building, and others were fitting this into place. Inside, the episcopal throne, decorated with a design of shamrocks, which hitherto had so intrigued me, was gone; so was the second of the twin altars which, when they rose at either end of the noble edifice, gave it so striking and so unique an aspect. But one of them was still intact, or almost intact; the part of the nave nearest it had been boarded off so that services could proceed normally; and when we had taken the narrow winding road—hardly more than a lane —which leads to the Bishop's House, I was admitted to the portal imbedded in the high wall by the same smiling nun who had welcomed us on previous visits. Beyond the blossoming garden, the door stood open into the pleasant parlor where nothing seemed changed; then presently the Bishop came in and, glory be! he seemed least changed of all!

He talked, at first gravely, and then with touches of typical Gaelic humor, about the German Occupation, which had lasted four years. During this time he had twice been on the point of deportation and twice had been reprieved at the last moment. There had been some good Catholics among the Germans and, "as far as they could" they had contrived to be helpful; indeed, they had not been unresourceful in finding inconspicuous ways of accomplishing their ends. A succession of commandants had been stationed at Nevers, with their headquarters at the Hôtel de France. Immediately after their arrival, each of these commandants had called formally upon the Bishop, accompanied by two aides. The following day, the Bishop had returned the call, accompanied by two priests. At this point, social relations had been broken off and, even before reaching it, conversations had been stiff, stilted and limited. On one occasion, after the United States had entered the war, the commandant asked the Bishop to state, confidentially, whether, in his opinion, it could win. "Why should it?" the Bishop countered. "After all, it did not begin warlike preparations until after the attack on Pearl Harbor and you began in 1933." The commandant cast a furious glance at the cleric and bowed himself out, followed by his two aides, also bowing. Amenities had ended even more abruptly than usual.

The bombing from the invading armies occurred on July 16, 1944—a beautiful, clear night when the Bishop was about to conduct services at the Church of Our Lady of Carmel. Two parochial schools—one for boys and one for girls—were destroyed, but the museum* acted as a screen for the Bishop's House. The railroad station was, as usual, the actual target; but—also as usual—the bombers missed it, though the Bishop said, rather wryly, that "The English did a better job of bombing than the

---

* This museum was formerly the Bishop's Palace but, in 1906, was appropriated by the civil government, in the course of one of those periodic crusades against church property which seem so peculiarly French. It appears rather like an example of poetic justice that this museum should have saved the much more modest dwelling to which the episcopal incumbent of that time had been obliged to retreat and where his successors have lived ever since.

Americans." In all, one hundred and sixty persons were killed at Nevers. The Germans hung on until September, but finally left "rather hurriedly." It was the haste of this departure that saved the Bishop from deportation the second time.

I told the Bishop how greatly I deplored the destruction of the shamrock throne; but, trying to match his genial mood, said I was grateful to see that the great clock with the performing figures, which emerge from its works when it strikes, was still standing in the nave, though apparently it had not yet been set in motion again. I had always enjoyed that clock; it is almost as unique an accessory to a French cathedral as the shamrocks. But of course that was just a detail; what was infinitely more important, there were still services. Ah, yes, the Bishop said, those went on now without interruption. They managed somehow; and he had faith that, given time and prayer, the cathedral would again rise in its former spaciousness and splendor toward the heavens. The little votive chapel where Bernadette had first been buried, and which had been destroyed by a bomb—that is, all of it except the slab which had marked her first resting place—well, that chapel might be rebuilt, too. There was a project, or at least a hope, of doing so as a thank offering on the Superior General's Golden Jubilee, soon to be celebrated.

Speaking of the Superior General, I had an appointment with her at eleven; I must take my leave of the Bishop and go on to the Motherhouse. Yes, he knew that I was expected. He would not detain me any longer. He had no suggestions to make for the revision of the biography. As he had said, when it first came out, it met with his unqualified approval. A new Foreword though, bringing it up to date? Well, perhaps that might be a good idea. But he hoped the story itself would remain unchanged, except in that it would be necessary to indicate that persons with whom I had talked on previous visits were now dead, and to mention in passing the destruction of the votive chapel. He would send the Sister who had met me at the gate to show me the way to the Motherhouse—it was so long since I had been there, I might have forgotten this. I should not allow so much time to elapse again without coming to Nevers, where I was very welcome. Yes indeed, he would give me his blessing—a blessing on me and on my work. I knelt to receive it, and went out into the blossoming garden. He summoned the Sister and himself accompanied me to my car. I left him, a noble figure, framed in the portal opening through the high wall.

Within a matter of minutes, I was ushered into another stately presence—that of the Reverend Mother Superior General, Marie Alphonse.* She received me in her small study, approached through an antechamber which leads from the arcade at the rear of the Motherhouse; and for a few minutes we sat talking about my previous visits, which she recalled with kindly courtesy, and about the purpose of my present one, which she assured me was pleasing to her. Then she suggested that we should visit the remains of the votive chapel together.

The arcade flanks a large landscaped garden, dominated by a central cross, where the Sisters spend much

---

* She should not be confused with my other old and valued friend, the Superior of the Hospital Bernadette at Lourdes. Their names in religion, by a curious coincidence, are the same—or perhaps I should say were the same, for the Superior of the Hospital Bernadette, who was so ill when I was at Lourdes, died before I reached Nevers.

of their recreation in favorable weather; this is easy to understand, for its trees afford pleasant shade, its flower beds are bright with bloom and there are well-ordered walks along which to stroll and convenient seats on which to rest. All this is situated on an elevation that forms a terrace above the kitchen garden, which is reached by the means of a long, easy incline. At a turn in this incline, I was surprised to see, in a niche, a statue of St. Teresa— not the little St. Thérèse of Lisieux, which would have astonished me less, but the great St. Teresa of Ávila. I told the Superior General that I had just come from Spain, that I had been briefly to Ávila and that I hoped to return there next year for seclusion and study—and, of course, for writing. So during the next few moments we spoke of that other mystic city, beyond the Pyrenees, which owes its fame to a saint, in a way very different from the one in which Lourdes owes its fame to Bernadette, but just as significantly, just as gloriously. And as we talked we walked along and came nearer and nearer to the ruins of the little chapel where Bernadette was first buried, and where nothing now remains but the slab which had marked her resting place.

There is something startling about that solitary slab, lying unblemished in the midst of the ruins, and in the final words of its deeply chiseled epitaph, which seems to have gained, rather than lost, in boldness.* We talked no more of any other place or any other saint as I stood gazing at them. But at last the Superior General said gently, "Remember, she is not there any more. Come,

---

* *C'est ici le lieu de mon repos:*   ("This is my resting-place forever,
   J'y habiterai parce que je l'ai choisi.   here will I dwell, for I have desired
           Ps. CXXXI, 14.   it. . . .")

let us go to the chapel where we will *really* find her. You have been there before, I know. But this time I am going to take you into the sanctuary itself, and we will pray together, close beside her."

Like the first experience at the grotto in Lourdes, so many years ago, this is one I shall never forget and, indeed, I believe that the revelation of Lourdes is incomplete unless it includes the revelation of Nevers. It is a source of astonishment to me that so few pilgrims seem to realize this. The chapel is never entirely empty—or so I believe—but there is a silence about the place, greater than the silence of any other church with which I am familiar, and it seemed more silent than ever on that day of which I am now speaking. Among the worshipers we passed, as we went up the aisle, were several young children of the type that are usually unruly; also, several husky, ruddy countrymen of the type who usually make a clumping sound as they move about, no matter how reverent they are and how quietly they try to walk; but this silence engulfed them, too. The Superior General opened the gate of the altar railing, and it made not the slightest sound as she did so. Then we entered the sanctuary side by side and, side by side, knelt near the coffin of gold and glass which encloses the figure of the saint, clad in her black habit, with her head resting lightly on a pillow and her fingers interlaced with her rosary. The figure, did I say? This is not a figure, in the sense that the word is so often used—that is to say, it is not an image. It is the saint herself.

*"Vous savez, c'est son corps,"** the Superior General whispered, and her hushed words seemed to reverberate

---
* "You know, that is her body."

xxxviii

in the silence. A bearded missionary priest, robed in brown, girdled with cord, who was the only other person in the sanctuary and who was kneeling at the farther end of the coffin, looked up quickly from his beads and looked quickly down again. He had heard the whisper, and though he had not needed the assurance—nor had I—the fact that the only words uttered in that place of peace were exactly those, seemed to me deeply moving, deeply significant. I shall remember them with emotion and thanksgiving as long as I live.

When we went out into the sunshine again, I heard a bell ringing and I knew, from long familiarity with the ways of convents, that the hour must be approaching when the Superior General should go to the Refectory. But when I said I did not think I should trespass further on her time, she put her hand on my arm.

"Before you go," she said, "let us stop in front of the grotto of Our Lady of Waters, in the courtyard—the statue there, you know, is the one which Bernadette insisted most resembled the 'Beautiful Lady' of her visions. I think it is fitting that you and I should now say a prayer that she will beatify your work."

Can I doubt that she will, after such a prayer in such a place?

PART ONE

The Shepherdess

✿ ONE ✿

A LITTLE girl sat among the sheep she was tending for her foster mother.

She had eaten the black bread which had been given her in the morning when she set out for the pasture, and also some fruit which a kindly neighbor had brought her since. Now she was not hungry any more; she played with a small lamb that gamboled about her as she watched the staid sheep. Some of these had green stripes down their backs. Once, when she was younger, her father, who had come up from Lourdes to see her, told her teasingly that such green stripes came from something the sheep had eaten. She had burst into tears, fearing that she had failed to observe some pernicious weed in the pasture. Now she knew better. She knew that the green stripe was the mark of the man who was to buy some of the sheep, and though her heart contracted at the thought of losing them, it was not troubled about their welfare.

The slope where the sheep were feeding was verdant and sunny. They moved slowly about, their bells tinkling as they munched. Except for the tinkling bells and the munching sheep, there was no sound. Some of the flock,

3

which had already eaten their fill, crouched comfortably in the shade of the trees with which the pasture was bordered. Beyond it were other pastures and fields. Some of the fields were planted with tall corn and thrifty potatoes. Others were hayfields. Where the grass was still standing, it was mingled with Queen Anne's lace, white and feathery, and red clover which gave forth a sweet scent. Where the grass had already been cut, there was the fragrance which comes from new-mown hay.

Beyond the pastures and the hayfields rose the mountains. The air was clear, and this made the outlines of the mountains clear, too. But along the skyline the summits were lightly veiled. The little girl did not know whether the clouds rested gently on them, forming this veil, or whether there had been a quiet snowfall, such as sometimes comes to the heights, even in summer. She only knew that they were beautiful and remote and mysterious, and she lifted up her eyes to them, as many centuries before another shepherd, who was a sweet singer as well, had lifted up his eyes to the hills of Israel which surrounded him, and whence, as he told in one of his songs, "came his help."

The little girl did not sing songs, except in her own soul. As she watched her sheep, she told her beads. Her rosary was always in her small brown hands. It was at one and the same time her most familiar and her most precious possession. She could not read, but she could recite. She recited now, under her breath.

"Hail, Mary, full of grace! Blessed art thou among women."

Presently, through the stillness, she heard the bells of the church in Bartrès, the village beyond the hollow, ringing the Angelus. The shadows began to lengthen across the sunny slope. It was time to take the sheep home. She glanced up to see if the small altar which she had made of pebbles garnered in the pasture, and decorated with field flowers she had found there, was still in perfect order. When she perceived that it was, she was content to leave it for the night. She rose tranquilly, and the dog which dozed beside her was instantly on the alert. He darted back and forth, driving the sheep before him. The little girl followed, her great dark eyes watchful as she walked, her pleasant, chubby face slightly serious. The path between the pasture and her foster mother's cottage was not an easy one. It was rough and stony, and bordered by thorny thickets. The little girl did not mind the stones and the thorns herself; she was used to a rough road. But she did not want her sheep to stumble or to feel the thorns through their thick fleece. She did not want them to hurt themselves.

There were not only the stones and the thorns to think of, there was also the brook. Sometimes it swelled suddenly. Once, when she had taken the sheep to their pasture in the morning, it was only a tiny trickling stream. But later in the day there had been a violent storm. When she tried to get the sheep back to shelter, she was confronted with a raging torrent. She did not know what to do, so she did what was natural to her under such circumstances: she made the sign of the cross and prayed. When she looked about her again, she saw that the torrent was not as great as it had seemed at first. It was apparently flowing in two different directions, and thus divided, it could be forded in safety. Later, when she glanced back at it, she thought that it was again impassable. But that

5

was not until the very last lamb had bounded over the bed of the brook.

Tonight there had been no trouble. There had been no storms during the day; it had been one of complete serenity. The little girl saw the sheep comfortably settled in their fold, and went herself to her foster mother's cottage, taking off her wooden shoes on the threshold. Like most of the buildings in the village, the cottage had only one story. It was overhung with vines and covered with a red tile roof. On either side of the door was a room with a huge fireplace at one end. All the cooking was done at the fireplace in the kitchen. (1) Between the fireplace and the wall stood the big bed draped with red and white checked curtains, where the little girl's foster mother, Marie Avarant, slept with her surly husband. Beyond, in a series of small niches under the window, stood the household vessels. Opposite the fireplace, against the farther wall, was the buffet which served as a larder, and the troughlike *pétrin* where bread was mixed. As the little girl came into the kitchen, Père Avarant spoke to her sharply, and Marie called to her to come and comfort a fretful child. The little girl took up the baby, soothed it in the same way that she "gentled" her lambs, and sat down in a low chair by the fire, holding the child cradled in her arms.

Her feelings were not hurt because she was ordered about. She knew that Père Avarant's bark was worse than his bite, and that Marie Avarant, who had suckled her when she was a baby, in the place of a child who had died, at heart loved her dearly. It had always been Marie's custom, whenever she came into Lourdes, to tuck a small present of some sort—a bunch of fragrant flowers, a rosy peach or a sweet cake—destined for the little girl, in the

6

basket which she carried over her arm. When eventually she suggested that she would like to take the child back to Bartrès with her, this caused the little girl no concern. On the contrary, Marie had always invited her for the Feast of St. John the Baptist and for the Carnival; and she had also gone to Bartrès of her own accord, several times each year, for the mere pleasure of being with the Avarant family. When Marie had suggested to her that she might stay for some time and help in the care of the younger children, she had consented gladly. Nor had she been distressed, on her arrival, to find that she was to tend the sheep instead. She loved all small, simple creatures. The more little and helpless they were, the more they appealed to her. Whether it was a lamb or a baby that she cosseted, her tenderness was the same.

Now she sat by the fireplace until the baby was fast asleep; then she laid it down and set about to make herself useful in other ways. But it was not work, primarily, that Marie Avarant required of her tonight. It was learning, and that came much harder. She had not been sent to school, though that had been part of the Bartrès bargain; she had been sent out with the sheep instead. So she had never acquired the familiar habit of books. She did not even speak or understand French, in which the books thereabouts were written. She spoke and understood only the Bigourdane dialect. However, her foster mother had also promised her parents that she should learn the catechism, and this pledge weighed more heavily on the peasant woman's mind than the other. She meant to keep it, come what might. So the little girl tried to repeat the long French sentences which her foster mother read aloud to her. But she could not remember them. They were not short and simple, like the *Aves* which she loved to say by herself, or like the touching stories which the village schoolmaster had sometimes told her, in patois, about Jesus and His mother.

Besides, she had been out all day in the open air with her sheep. She was drowsy now, and this drowsiness made her seem stupid. She could hardly keep her eyes open, much less keep her wits about her. She was startled when she saw Marie Avarant fling away the catechism book, and heard her exclaim, "Go on, what is the use? You will never be anything but an ignorant little fool!" But she did not retort, though a quick reply always rose readily enough to her lips. Instead, she got up, and putting her arms around her foster mother's neck, kissed her gently on the cheek. Then she retreated quietly to the corner where she could lie down in her own little bed, coughing a little as she went. She conscientiously tried to stifle the cough, lest it should disturb the younger children who were already asleep. She took off the striped kerchief which had covered her black hair, and the shawl which had been folded neatly across her slim shoulders and young breast. She was tidy in all her habits. When she was ready for the night, she knelt down one last time, asking that Mary, full of grace and blessed among women, should watch over her and pray for her—then and in the hour of her death. Afterward she settled herself for rest, her rosary still between her fingers.

No one who has followed her story from start to finish can doubt that her prayer was answered.

8

Photograph by Peter Bowen Keyes

STATUE OF SAINT BERNADETTE IN THE CLINIC GARDEN

Photograph by Margaretta M. Keyes

THE CATHEDRAL OF ST. CYR AT NEVERS BEFORE AND AFTER
THE BOMBING IN 1944

❊ TWO ❊

THE LITTLE girl whom we found tending her flock on the hillside near Bartrès was a young Bigourdane peasant, named Marie Bernarde Soubirous. Her father, François Soubirous, had once been the proud possessor of a mill in the Lapaca quarter of Lourdes. But he had lost it. He was a good-natured, easygoing man, who gave more credit than he could get, and did not worry when he could not make both ends meet. His manner was sometimes surly, and so was his speech, in spite of his essential conviviality; this surliness was naturally not conducive to trade. Moreover, he did not always send his flour out promptly, or in perfect condition. In a word, he was slack. His thrifty customers resented this trait.

The mill had been part of his wife's dowry, and if she had possessed the frugality and prudence usually so typical of the French, her inheritance might have been saved for her children in spite of François. But Louise Soubirous had much the same sort of characteristics and habits as her husband. Though she was sharp tongued with her children, she was gregarious and largehearted; not one of the neighbors who brought grain to the mill

9

to be ground left it without being urged to break bread there. The day inevitably came when the larder, so generously kept open, became empty.

It is easy to re-create family life in the small house, of which the mill itself was an integral part. At the left of the entrance was the beamed kitchen, with its large open fireplace, its primitive cooking utensils and its conjugal bed, draped with red and white striped cotton, standing in one corner—a kitchen differing in no essential way from the Avarants' at Bartrès—and from hundreds of other Basque kitchens for that matter, except that it was less large and light. It was in this room that Louise gave birth to her first child, a little girl, on the seventh of January, 1844, amid the general rejoicing that so happy an event entails; and two days later the baby was christened in the parish church (2) and given in baptism the name of Marie Bernarde, though from the beginning she was familiarly called Bernadette.

She was still a baby herself when she was crowded out of her cradle by the arrival of a little brother Jean; and it was during this period that she was first sent to Bartrès to be nursed by Marie Avarant. The first Jean did not live long, and neither did two younger brothers who bore the same name. But other babies came thick and fast: Toinette Marie, who became her elder sister's closest companion; Justin, Bernard Pierre and still one more Jean. The little girls slept together in a bed at the front of the room over the kitchen; the little boys slept in two beds in the rear of the same room. There were checked curtains between, a fireplace, two straight-backed chairs and the indispensable *armoire,* which dominates all other furnishings in a French house, serving at one and the same

10

time as wardrobe, closet and linen press. The stone floor was bare. The one window gave little light. To most of us it would seem a poor place. But the Soubirous were happy to have such a home. They were overwhelmed with disaster when they lost it.

Having forfeited the mill for debt, their fortunes sank lower and lower. They drifted aimlessly from one miserable tenement to another. François and Louise both went out by the day when they could get work, leaving the younger children in charge of Bernadette. But often there was no work to be had, and by-and-by there was no money to rent even the most squalid sort of lodging. It had never been the way of the Soubirous to ask for charity. But finally, in desperation, François appealed to one Andre Sajous, a relative of his wife's, asking for permission to take shelter in a building which Sajous owned in the rue des Petits Fossés, a building which had once served as the local jail and which, on this account, was commonly called *Le Cachot*.

The building contained only two rooms. Sajous, who was a stone mason, used the front room, facing the street, as his atelier; but the dark little back room was empty, and the Soubirous family was grudgingly permitted to move in there. They brought with them the linen and the furniture which they had salvaged from the general wreckage: those hand-woven sheets, coarse and cool, which form part of the humblest French girl's trousseau; those solid chests which are handed down from one generation to another by the poorest peasants. The quarters in the mill had been spacious compared to *Le Cachot*—indeed, it becomes a matter of wonder how this could have contained more than the four curtained beds—also providentially saved—one of which was placed in each corner, or how any kind of organized living could have taken place there. Yet more than one contemporary states that "Louise Soubirous liked to keep things clean and brought her children up well." Their threadbare clothes were never tattered; these were so neatly patched and mended that the youngsters always looked tidy and trim in them. The secret of their mother's success doubtless lay in the fact that she strove to preserve the decencies, not only in her habits but also in her feelings.(3)

Lacking money to buy food, Louise did little or no cooking; a kind of coarse corn bread constituted the family's staple nourishment. But because Bernadette was a delicate little girl, because her mother recognized how woefully inadequate this was for her, Louise Soubirous occasionally managed somehow to bring home a small white loaf destined to be kept apart for her eldest daughter and given to her in morsels soaked with wine and sweetened with sugar. But the inevitable happened: the younger children crowded around their sister, clamoring for their share, and she gave it to them. Half a loaf is admittedly better than no bread, but a loaf divided into five or six pieces does very little to appease anyone's hunger. At a pitifully early age, Bernadette learned the hard lesson of renunciation. Her knowledge unlocked the door to the steep and narrow path which leads to perfection.

In so far as it was possible for her, she took touching care to see that none of her brothers and sisters suffered from hunger as much as she did. An aged peasant of Bartrès, Mère Poueyto, always hugged to her heart an episode which occurred when Bernadette was about

12

twelve years old, and sometimes she was persuaded to tell it:

She and her husband were the proud possessors of a field where the cemetery now stands, and they hired Louise Soubirous and two other women to reap it for them. Women reapers at this period were paid twenty cents a day, or slightly less "by the piece," which was the way Louise was hired to do the backbreaking work which she so thankfully accepted. She left *Le Cachot* at dawn and did not return to it until dark.

One morning between nine and ten, Mère Poueyto was startled to see her open doorway darkened by a little girl who was holding a baby in her arms. The child had a cheap cotton handkerchief folded over dark hair and wore the customary crossed shawl, ankle-length dress and wooden shoes. She looked very tired. Her great velvety eyes were ringed with fatigue and her slender figure was bowed by its burden. But she smiled as she said politely, "Madame, will you tell me where to find your field? I must take my little brother to my mother, so that he can be nursed."

"How old is your little brother?" the peasant woman asked her small visitor.

"Six months."

Mère Poueyto knew that the case was urgent. Since Louise had no choice but to leave him behind when she went to work, the baby had not been fed for hours. The peasant woman told her daughter Romaine to show Bernadette the way to the field at once.

As they went along they met a neighbor who was carrying soup to the reapers. At that place and period, the peasants' breakfast, which they ate as soon as they were

13

awake, consisted of a single piece of bread spread with salt and garlic. They were ravenously hungry for their midmorning soup and watched eagerly for its coming. It sustained them until their meager two o'clock dinner. After that there was nothing more to eat except a thin corn soup, potatoes and some cheese at nightfall.

Romaine entrusted Bernadette and the baby to the soup carrier and left them. The others went on. When they found the reapers, Louise made a shelter from a stack and nursed the baby under a canopy of ripening wheat. Bernadette sat on the warm stubbly ground beside her mother, looking off at the mountains. She rested. Then she picked the baby up again and started back to *Le Cachot.* After that she found her way to the field herself.

The winter of 1855 was a terribly bitter one. Cold stalked through the Pyrenees and the sufferings of the poor were redoubled—there was neither fire nor food among them. Bernadette's Aunt Casterot, who was also her godmother, took the little girl away from *Le Cachot* and kept the child in her own home for a few months. This was the best she could do for her. After that Bernadette went back again to the dark little room that she shared with her parents, her sister and her brothers and stayed there until she left for Bartrès, two years later— where we first found her.

From the viewpoint of physical welfare she was indubitably far better off in the mountain village, where the air was clear and clean and the coarse food adequate, than she was while abiding in *Le Cachot* of unrelieved gloom and want in the rue des Petits Fossés. But as she sat on the

14

high hillside, fingering her beads and watching her sheep, she became increasingly conscious of spiritual hunger and of yearning for divine light. She had not been reared in an atmosphere which could be called irreligious, strictly speaking. Family prayers had somehow been said, in unison, with surprising regularity; attendance at church had also been taken as a matter of course, and Louise and François had never failed to make their Paschal confession and receive their Easter Communion. Their daughter had perceived the solace and support that this seemed to give them. She was in her fourteenth year now, and with the normal emotional awakening of adolescence came another awakened awareness. She could not choose but heed it. She asked to be allowed to return to Lourdes in order that she herself might be properly prepared to make her First Communion.

At first she voiced the request indirectly. From her hillside pasture she saw a Lourdes acquaintance passing by and ran down the road to meet him. "Please ask my parents to come and fetch me," she said pleadingly. "I am not contented here." She had always been so easily contented that he might well have been warned there was some underlying reason for her restlessness. But either he forgot to tell Louise and François their daughter's desire, or they themselves belittled it. They did not come to get her. She waited a reasonable length of time for them to appear and then asked her foster father for permission to leave her flock and start off by herself. She said she wanted to stay in Lourdes for a few days, and since her absence entailed no great inconvenience at the moment, she was allowed to depart. She returned when she had promised, but only to say good-by. "I must go home," she told them

15

quietly but determinedly. "Monsieur le Curé is about to prepare his classes at the Hospice for their First Communion. If I am there, I can make mine with the others." The next morning she had disappeared.

It may very reasonably be asked why the Abbé Ader, the vicar of Bartrès, had not attended to her religious instruction, why she felt obliged to go to the Abbé Pomian instead. The vicar had not overlooked her. Indeed, one day he had seen her pass by with her sheep when he was out walking with Monsieur Barbet, the village schoolmaster, and had remarked, "That little shepherdess is exactly like what I have always imagined the children of the Salette(4) to have been." The comparison was perceptive and prophetic and revealed his remarkable gifts. But though he recognized the child as one apart, he was deceived as to her age. She was so small and slight that he supposed her to be much younger than she actually was. Moreover, his mind was preoccupied with a project of his own, which he had long hoped to see realized and which at length was on the verge of fulfillment. He was about to leave Bartrès to enter the Benedictine Order. He did indeed tell Marie Avarant that as Bartrès might be left for some time without a curé after his departure, he thought Bernadette should be sent to Lourdes for the instruction which he tardily realized he had been remiss in not giving her himself. But apparently this message also went astray. It seems certain that she acted on her own initiative in leaving Bartrès.

It was to the Hospice of Lourdes that she betook herself on a bleak day in early January. This institution served as a small supplementary home for the aged, giving shelter to twenty or thirty indigent old men and women for
16

whom a larger institution did not have room. But it had for its primary purpose at the time the education of young girls by the Sisters of Charity and Christian Instruction, whose lives are dedicated to the dual cause which their name implies, and whose Motherhouse was—and still is —at Nevers. Five hundred pupils, divided into three groups, were gathered together within the venerable walls of the Hospice. There was, first of all, a free elementary school for children whose parents could afford to give them nothing more substantial in the way of an education; there was a day school, with advanced as well as elementary classes, for pupils of more cultured and comfortable background; and there was a boarding school for girls who lived at a distance. The Sisters who taught them were devout and dignified women, with high standards of learning and living, and the setting for their school was both noble and charming. The façade of the main building was ornamented by a deep arcade, where flowers bloomed between tall columns of stone, and in the rear, double galleries, open to the friendly southern sun, looked out upon a sheltered garden. Inside, the long corridors were clean and cool, the rooms spacious and high studded. In the main drawing room was a square piano of the best make and latest mode, a great walnut secretary that reached almost to the ceiling, a gray marble mantel surmounted with appropriate ornaments, and armchairs and sofas of graceful design, upholstered in red velvet. The Sisters were proud of their parlor, as well they might be; but their little chapel, where a beautiful Virgin of painted wood, clothed in golden robes, surmounted the altar, was the shrine of their most consecrated joy.

Such a center as the Hospice and such preceptors as the

17

Sisters could not fail to make a deep impression on the youthful mind. Bernadette was strongly stirred by her initial experience there. She attended the elementary school, going back and forth to *Le Cachot* night and morning; and along with her catechism she began to acquire the rudiments of secular education. On most points she did not have a retentive memory, a fact which made the later exceptions to this rule more noticeable; and she never became adept at figures of any sort. On the other hand, she learned to read without difficulty and, before long, to write a beautiful flowing script and to express herself with delicacy and precision on paper no less than by word of mouth. Her diary is a notable document. She never became intellectual; the abstract and the speculative did not draw her. She liked practical facts and a well-ordered routine, and these she attacked intelligently. Her skill with the needle was remarkable, and she delighted in fine sewing, in embroidery and in the making of beautiful lace; the use of her hands came naturally to her. Probably she was never told that such a gift invariably has a steadying and tranquilizing effect, or never realized that it was in a sense akin to her instinctive resort to her rosary. Unversed in theories, unqualified for ritualistic orisons, her handicraft and her prayers formed part of the same exquisite and appointed pattern.

There are certain words in the English language which are gladly used by those whose work is in words, both because of their euphony and because of their beautiful meaning. One of these words is "splendor" and another is "modesty." It makes me happy to use both these words in writing about Bernadette. She had splendor of spirit and modesty of manner. Though she belonged to a class and

18

a time not notable for fastidious habits of cleanliness, she was always immaculate in her person. But she was not a prim little girl. She had the courage of her convictions, and she steadfastly clung to them, in the face of all opposition. As we have already seen, she could, upon occasion, take matters capably into her own hands; through her natural docility also ran a strong strain of roguishness and a habit of ready resort to repartee. One day she smuggled some snuff, which had been prescribed for her cough, into the schoolroom, and had the whole class sneezing before anyone could imagine what had caused such a sudden epidemic of bad colds. Her own troublesome asthma did not depress her. Even on her deathbed she mimicked the doctor, to the delight of her fellow invalids, and mischievously suggested to a Bishop that he should pick up his own skullcap, when he had allowed this to fall on the counterpane for the transparent purpose of making her touch it. She was never averse to a joke or at loss for a retort.

She remained small of stature and was not noticeably pretty, but she had a very winning and pleasing personality. "She is attractive," asserted the novices at the Motherhouse in Nevers—those "Little Bonnets" to whom she was so much attached herself—when, some years later, they were asked why they like to spend so much time in her company. The same description fitted her when she was fourteen. She was always smiling, always good natured. Her skin was clear and rosy. Her generous mouth was as expressive as her big black eyes, which were her most beautiful feature; they were soft, but they were searching and there was a sparkle in them. Her voice was surprisingly rich and full, issuing, as it did, from such an insignificant source. Her manner was courteous and cordial—she had innate refinement and the "candor of innocence." Her fellow pupils and her teachers all liked her. In a word, she was popular. During the six months which elapsed between her precipitate departure from Bartrès and her First Communion, her development in the auspicious atmosphere of the Hospice would have been rapid under any circumstances. But the circumstances which actually arose did much more than expand her consciousness; they transfigured her existence.

❉ THREE ❉

BERNADETTE could not spend all her time in school. One of her regular tasks was to glean stray branches that had fallen by the side of the river Gave, which flows through Lourdes—branches that had been overlooked by less provident and more prosperous persons, but that might serve her family as pitiful fuel. In wintertime it was doubly necessary that she should gather as many of such fagots as she could. There was nothing else to burn at *Le Cachot*.

At the point where the waters of the Gave and the old canal of Savy met and merged, there was a dark grotto of strange porous rock, partially covered by clumps of dwarf plants, and indented at one point above the vault which formed its interior by a small oval opening. There was an ancient legend saying that "a great wonder would some-day be wrought at Massabielle," as this place was called, but apparently the last thing that anyone wanted was to have this come to pass. The grotto was remote and repelling, surrounded by superstitions and shunned as sinister. No one voluntarily went there, though fishermen caught out in a storm sometimes took refuge there, and so did

21

shepherds who were compelled to find sudden shelter for their sheep. But the little shepherdess of Bartrès had never been driven to doing so in the course of her own herding. It was the necessity for finding firewood that finally took her there.

The story of what happened when she went has been told a thousand times in a thousand ways. I think it is best to give it in the way Bernadette told it herself, to a friend. She did this repeatedly, and it never varied in the telling(5):

"The Thursday before Ash Wednesday(6) it was cold and the weather was threatening. After our dinner my mother told us that there was no more wood in the house and she was vexed. My sister Toinette and I, to please her, offered to go and pick up dry branches by the riverside. My mother said 'no' because the weather was bad and we might be in danger of falling into the Gave. Jeanne Abadie, our neighbor and friend, who was looking after her little brother in our house and who wanted to come with us, took her brother back to his house and returned the next moment telling us that she had leave to come with us. My mother still hesitated, but seeing that there were three of us she let us go. We took first of all the road which leads to the cemetery, by the side of which wood is unloaded and where shavings can sometimes be found. That day we found nothing there. We came down by the side which leads near the Gave and, having arrived at Pont Vieux, we wondered if it would be best to go up or down the river. We decided to go down and, taking the forest road, we arrived at Merlasse. There we went into Monsieur de la Fitte's field by the mill of Savy. As soon as we had reached the end of this field, nearly opposite the

22

grotto of Massabielle, we were stopped by the canal of the mill we had just passed. The current of this canal was not strong for the mill was not working, but the water was cold and I for my part was afraid to go in. Jeanne Abadie and my sister, less timid than I, took their sabots in their hand and crossed the stream. However, when they were on the other side, they called out that it was cold and bent down to rub their feet and warm them. All this increased my fear, and I thought that if I went into the water I should get an attack of asthma. So I asked Jeanne Abadie, who was bigger and stronger than I, to take me on her shoulders.

" 'I should think not,' answered Jeanne; 'you're a mollycoddle; if you won't come, stay where you are.'

"After the others had picked up some pieces of wood under the grotto they disappeared along the Gave. When I was alone I threw some stones into the bed of the river to give me a foothold, but it was of no use. So I had to make up my mind to take off my sabots and and cross the canal as Jeanne and my sister had done.

"I had just begun to take off my first stocking when suddenly I heard a great noise like the sound of a storm. I looked to the right, to the left, under the trees of the river, but nothing moved; I thought I was mistaken. I went on taking off my shoes and stockings; then I heard a fresh noise like the first. I was frightened and stood straight up. I lost all power of speech and thought when, turning my head toward the grotto, I saw at one of the openings of the rock a rosebush, one only, moving as if it were very windy. Almost at the same time there came out of the interior of the grotto a golden-colored cloud, and soon after a Lady, young and beautiful, exceedingly beautiful, the like of whom I had never seen, came and placed herself at the entrance of the opening above the rosebush. She looked at me immediately, smiled at me and signed to me to advance, as if she had been my mother. All fear had left me but I seemed to know no longer where I was. I rubbed my eyes, I shut them, I opened them; but the Lady was still there continuing to smile at me and making me understand that I was not mistaken. Without thinking of what I was doing, I took my rosary in my hands and went on my knees. The Lady made a sign of approval with her head and herself took into her hands a rosary which hung on her right arm. When I attempted to begin the rosary and tried to lift my hand to my forehead, my arm remained paralyzed, and it was only after the Lady had signed herself that I could do the same. *The Lady left me to pray all alone; she passed the beads of her rosary between her fingers but she said nothing; only at the end of each decade did she say the 'Gloria' with me.*(7)

"When the recitation of the rosary was finished, the lady returned to the interior of the rock and the golden cloud disappeared with her.

"As soon as the Lady had disappeared Jeanne Abadie and my sister returned to the grotto and found me on my knees in the same place where they had left me. They laughed at me, called me imbecile and bigot, and asked me if I would go back with them or not. I had now no difficulty in going into the stream, and I felt the water as warm as the water for washing plates and dishes.

" 'You had no reason to make such an outcry,' I said to Jeanne and Marie while drying my feet; 'the water of the canal is not so cold as you seemed to make believe!'

" 'You are very fortunate not to find it so; we found it very cold.'

24

THE GARDEN OF THE CONVENT OF ST. GILDARD

THE GROTTO OF OUR LADY OF WATERS IN THE COURTYARD
OF THE CONVENT OF ST. GILDARD

"We bound up in three fagots the branches and fragments of wood which my companions had brought; then we climbed the slope of Massabielle and took the forest road. Whilst we were going toward the town I asked Jeanne and Marie if they had noticed anything at the grotto.

" 'No,' they answered. 'Why do you ask us?'

" 'Oh, nothing,' I replied indifferently.

"However, before we got to the house, I told my sister Marie of the extraordinary things which had happened to me at the grotto, asking her to keep it secret.

"Throughout the whole day the image of the Lady remained in my mind. In the evening at the family prayer I was troubled and began to cry.

" 'What is the matter?' asked my mother.

"Marie hastened to answer for me and I was obliged to give the account of the wonder which had come to me that day.

" 'These are illusions,' answered my mother; 'you must drive these ideas out of your head and especially not go back again to Massabielle.'

"We went to bed but I could not sleep. The face of the Lady, so good and so gracious, returned incessantly to my memory, and it was useless to recall what my mother had said to me; I could not believe that I had been deceived."

She could not believe that she had been deceived; the mental image which she had carried away with her from the grotto was by no means vague. She not only insisted that she had seen a "Beautiful Lady"; she described this beautiful lady minutely:

"She has the appearance of a young girl of sixteen or seventeen. She is dressed in a white robe, girdled at the waist with a blue ribbon which flows down all around it.

25

A yoke closes it in graceful pleats at the base of the neck; the sleeves are long and tight-fitting. She wears upon her head a veil which is also white; this veil gives just a glimpse of her hair and then falls down at the back below her waist. Her feet are bare but covered by the last folds of her robe except at the point where a yellow rose shines upon each of them. She holds on her right arm a rosary of white beads with a chain of gold shining like the two roses on her feet."

Bernadette was naturally eager to seek out this radiant vision again. She took her mother's sharp order not to return to the grotto deeply to heart and wept bitterly as she said her prayers that night. During the next few days she did not regain her customary cheerfulness. Louise, unaccustomed to seeing her so subdued, became increasingly alarmed and increasingly vociferous. She talked incessantly about the deceptiveness of illusions and the beauty in which evil often disguises itself. Bernadette listened to her politely and patiently. Ready as she was with repartee, she did not reply to her mother's tirade, and this was another disquieting sign. Louise did not know how to cope with it and, in despair, finally gave up trying. Meanwhile, Bernadette quietly continued to think things over.

She did not believe that she was the victim of an illusion any more than she believed she had been deceived. Everything had been so real to her—the fitful wind, the swaying shrubs, the golden light, the Beautiful Lady. And she saw no reason why the devil, little as she knew of him, should wish to recite a rosary or choose to do so in the grotto of Massabielle. She kept her own counsel, but the more she reflected, the more certain she became that she was right and her mother mistaken. By Sunday(8) she was so sure of this and so eager to go back to the grotto in the hope of seeing the Beautiful Lady again that she asked her sister and her friend Jeanne Abadie to intercede for her and obtain permission from her mother to do so.

At first Louise angrily refused to grant this permission, but eventually she decided that after all she was making a mountain out of a molehill, that it might be best to let the little girl go. If she saw nothing this time she would be abashed; she would get over her obstinacy and forget her foolish fancies. Louise's consent made her conviction of this clear.

Armed with her defiant permission and equipped with a phial of Holy Water, which they had decided to use if her dire predictions were true after all, the three little girls set out at last for the grotto by way of the forest road. They were quickly joined by half a dozen others; several more who wanted to come announced that they would be along very soon, but they thought they had better change their dresses first, as it was Sunday and all. They begged Jeanne Abadie to wait for them, which she agreed to do. Bernadette herself had not told anyone except her family about her Thursday's experience; but Toinette, who had not the same gift for keeping her own counsel, had prattled about it all over the quarter. The result was widespread curiosity and interest. Bernadette was quite indifferent to this. All her thoughts were still centered upon the Beautiful Lady, and she hurried blindly on. As soon as she had arrived at Massabielle, she knelt down at the right of the grotto, opposite the wild rosebush, and began to pray, while the group that was with her waited breathlessly to see what would happen. They saw nothing at all.

27

But they were conscious of a strange tension in the air; and almost immediately Bernadette called to them.

"There she is! There she is!"

The precious phial had been entrusted to a little girl named Marie Hillot. She slipped it quickly into Bernadette's hands, crying out excitedly:

"Throw the water! Throw it at her quickly!"

Bernadette took the bottle and obediently poured out its contents. But she herself was neither excited nor dismayed. She turned to her friends long enough to tell them that the Beautiful Lady did not seem displeased—that, on the contrary, she was smiling very sweetly, as if she approved of what had been done. Then Bernadette appeared to forget the other children entirely.

They knelt down in a semicircle around her, looking, in a troubled way, first at the oval above them where they themselves could see nothing but a rosebush, and then at their close companion, who had suddenly become apart. They could not understand her quick withdrawal and her enraptured gaze into space. It frightened them. Several of them began to cry, and one sobbed out, "Suppose Bernadette should die!"

The idea gave them fresh food for fright, and just then a stone, mysteriously dislodged from the top of a hill, came bounding down the rock and splashed into the river. They were panic stricken. They leaped up and fled in every direction, screaming for help as they ran. When they reached the forest road again, the mystery of the falling stone was explained: Jeanne Abadie, arriving on the scene with the vain late-comers, had thrown it herself, for fun. She was convulsed with laughter at their senseless fear. But the harm had already been done. The mother and sister of Nicolau, the miller of Savy, had heard the children's cries, and deciding that evil must have indeed befallen them, had also rushed to Massabielle. Terrified in their own turn by Bernadette's trancelike state, they hurried back to the mill to fetch Nicolau himself. He came, skeptically and sarcastically, but in the end proved the most sympathetic and understanding of anyone in the hysterical group. He lifted Bernadette gently to her feet and guided her back to the mill, speaking to her soothingly as they went along. The other children had continued their headlong flight back to town and Toinette had burst in upon her mother, sobbing unintelligibly. Louise could make no sense of her incoherence, and more and more irritated, she flung out of the house determined to sift the matter to the bottom this time. Two neighbors whom she met on the road told her that there had been much ado about nothing and that Bernadette was now resting quietly at Nicolau's house. But she was far from being placated. She rushed on to the mill, snatching up a switch as she went. She was angry through and through.

As soon as she saw her daughter she began to berate her bitterly. She would have belabored her also, if Nicolau and his mother had not interfered. They told her she should as soon think of striking an angel as of beating Bernadette. Far from being terrified, like the children, they had been tremendously touched by what they had seen. They did not understand Bernadette's trancelike state, from which she was slowly beginning to emerge, but they were moved to respect and awe by it. Little by little they succeeded in calming Louise, and they would not suffer the mother and daughter to depart until some sort of family peace had been restored. But this was bound to

29

be short lived. The entire neighborhood had now become aroused. Part of it jeered; part of it trembled; all of it was puzzled, piqued and overwrought.

Bernadette would certainly have suffered in this super-charged atmosphere if a young lady of assured position and charming manner, Antoinette Peyret, had not found a pretext for coming to *Le Cachot* at this time. Antoinette had been as greatly impressed by what she had heard as Nicolau by what he had seen; like the miller, she wanted to talk with the child herself, and something about her gracious presence proved disarming. Bernadette's reserve and her parents' antagonism alike melted away. Unrebuked, the little girl spoke with obvious sincerity about her two experiences at the grotto, which she outlined as almost identical; and when she described the dress that the Beautiful Lady had worn, she saw that her visitor was much moved.

As a matter of fact, Antoinette Peyret had reached a conclusion of her own regarding the mysterious apparition, and she felt that Bernadette's description confirmed her conviction: a short time before, the local branch of the Children of Mary had lost its adored president, Elisa Latapie, who had been one of Antoinette's dearest friends. There was universal mourning over her death, but no one except her immediate family was more grief stricken than Antoinette. Now, in her sorrowful state, she felt half hopeful and half fearful that Elisa's gentle spirit had revealed itself, clad in the traditional blue and white of the Children of Mary, and that its return might indicate a desire for prayer in its behalf. After Antoinette had left *Le Cachot,* she confided her thoughts to Madame Millet, another friend who had known and loved Elisa, and sug-

30

gested that they should go back to the Soubirous' hovel together. She would not rest now until she saw the apparition herself, and she was certain that Bernadette—and Bernadette alone—could guide her to it.

They reached *Le Cachot* opportunely. Louise had begun to berate Bernadette again, and at first she was anything but pleased to find that her visitors not only intended to encourage another visit to the grotto, but also desired to go there themselves. Angrily, she accused them of wishing to make a laughingstock out of her child. Speaking sharply in her own turn, Madame Millet warned her not to be insulting. Louise had reached a point where the reproof did her good. She had sense enough to see that it was a very different matter to entrust Bernadette to these two gentlewomen than to turn her loose with a crowd of young hoodlums. She gave her respectful consent to the venture.

The three must have made a picturesque procession. They started out very early in the morning,(9) before the full light of day. Madame Millet and Mademoiselle Peyret had come knocking softly at the Soubirous' door in the darkness; and Bernadette, who was eagerly waiting for them, lying wide awake beside her sleeping sister, had slipped silently out to join them. Almost no one saw them, for almost no one was abroad at this hour. As they walked through the hushed streets, a bell rang out, announcing the first Mass, and they went into the church whence the sound came. It was almost empty also, and their prayers were doubly devout because they were undisturbed. When they emerged and took the road to Massabielle, Bernadette led the way, a sturdy and sure-footed little figure, substantial in the vaporous gloom. Madame Millet

31

came next, carrying in her hand the traditional taper of Candlemas, which had been blessed at the time of that feast, and which since then she had lighted in her own home on other festivals or at moments which seemed to her especially portentous; it scarcely flickered as she moved forward now, holding it openly between her fingers. Antoinette's hands, on the contrary, were hidden beneath the folds of a black-hooded Pyrenean cloak in which she was wrapped; she held a sheet of paper, a pen and a small bottle of ink. It was her hope that if the vision spoke again, its words might be accurately recorded.

Unconsciously, the little leader had quickened her pace. She was already on her knees, reciting her rosary opposite the oval recess where the wild rose grew, when her two companions reached the grotto. They knelt down in their turn, and in their turn began to pray. Almost immediately they were startled by hearing Bernadette exclaim in a glad voice, "There she is again!" When they looked in the direction she indicated, they themselves could see nothing. But they were not disheartened. They continued to pray, confident that if they were right concerning the identity of the vision, their prayers would be acceptable; and when they had finished, they handed the paper and pen to Bernadette, begging her to ask the Beautiful Lady whether there was anything she wished to tell them, and whether, if there was, she would not be so good as to write it down.

Bernadette was not in the trancelike state which had frightened the children a few days before. She looked contented, but not ecstatic; and she was completely collected. She accepted the writing materials without objection and took a few steps forward, motioning to the others to re-
32

main behind; then she raised the paper and pen in the direction of the rosebush. For a few moments she appeared to be listening attentively to something that was being said to her. Then she lowered her arms, curtsied deeply and turned back to the two women who were anxiously awaiting her words.

"The Beautiful Lady told me it was not necessary to write down what she had to say to me. But she has asked me if I would come here, regularly, for fifteen days."

"What did you answer?"

"I told her I would."

"But why does she want you to come?"

"I don't know. She didn't tell me."

"Why did you make us a sign just now to stay back when you went forward?"

"In obedience to the Beautiful Lady."

"Oh! Is our presence distasteful to her? Please ask her!"

They were genuinely distressed at having intruded. But Bernadette reassured them.

"No. It isn't distasteful. She says so herself."

They were reassured, but they did not try to approach closely a second time. They passed an hour in prayer. However, though they were devout, they were not absorbed, and they noticed that Bernadette's own devotions seemed to be intermittent. Every now and then she appeared to be communing, rather than praying. When she rejoined them, they asked her eagerly if anything additional had been told her.

"Yes. The Beautiful Lady has said that she does not promise that I will be happy in this world, but that I shall be in the next."

❀ FOUR ❀

SHE WAS not wholly happy. Those who observed her closely at the time describe her as "half sorrowful, half joyous," which was entirely natural. She had not had a chance to assimilate the astonishing experiences she had undergone. Until she could do this, she could hardly seem glad in a buoyant way. But what she lacked in exuberance she made up in purpose; she succeeded in convincing both her parents and her godmother that she should be permitted to return, without interference, to the grotto.

Her mother and her aunt now went there with her. So did crowds of ever-increasing size. She always returned to exactly the same spot, and no one attempted to usurp this. "That is Bernadette's own place," the people said, drawing back so that she might take it in peace; and some of those who saw her tried to describe her as she looked when she was in a trance to those who had not. "She was beautiful," they said; "not with the sort of fresh rosiness that makes us smile when we see a child that has it, but with a strange exalted loveliness. She was pale, but there was a translucence to her pallor, as if it were lighted from within. She kept her eyes open, and she seemed to look

34

with joy and fascination toward some distant radiance. Sometimes her lips moved very slightly, but for the most part she kept them quietly closed. Her whole face was illumined as if with a reflection of bliss. But occasionally two large tears fell from her eyes and glistened on her cheeks."(10)

This picture is so different from the one which represents Bernadette as a cheerful, tidy child, comely rather than charming, that it is all the more striking by way of contrast. Among the persons who watched her at Massabielle, and who described her afterward, were numerous scholars, scientists and trained observers. There is not the slightest reason to doubt the accuracy of their impressions.

The first scientist who "came to scoff and remained to pray" was a well-known physician of Lourdes, Dr. Dozous; the first "prominent citizen" was Monsieur Estrade, an official in the Government Bureau of *Contributions Indirectes*, which, in France, cares for such items as the taxes levied on salt, sugar, tobacco and the like. The doctor performed an immediate service by testifying that from the medical standpoint there was nothing in the least abnormal about Bernadette while she was in a trancelike state: "Her pulse was regular, her respiration easy, and nothing indicated any nervous excitement."(11) Monsieur Estrade performed a later and even more valuable service. He kept a minute account of all the sights he saw and all the conversations he heard which concerned Bernadette. He was living quietly in Lourdes with his unmarried sister when the phenomena occurred, in an apartment on the second floor of the house where Monsieur Jacomet, the Commissioner of Police, had an apartment on the first floor. Their home was the center of much pleasant hospitality, and the nature of Monsieur Estrade's work brought him into contact with almost everyone in town, from the highest to the lowest degrees. He knew the Soubirous family well, and encouraged them all, including Bernadette, to talk to him candidly, which they did again and again. The clergy and magistrates of the town also conferred with him freely over a long period of years. The records that he left of these conferences and various others, eventually assembled in book form at the request of Cardinal Langenieux, late Archbishop of Rheims, forms one of the most valuable documents of its sort in existence, and I have ventured to draw on them freely, for they furnish the clearest version I have found of the obstacles with which the little shepherdess was called upon to contend.

By the twenty-first of February, when the sixth apparition took place, the town fathers were beginning to feel some concern about the mysterious events which were causing such a furor in their quiet little center, and they met in the Mayor's office to see what steps they had better take to put an end to them. The meeting was not wholly harmonious. Those who believed in the visions and those who did not exchanged sharp words; it was evident that if a small group of thoughtful and intelligent men could become heated on the subject, an ignorant and excited crowd, under the spell of mass psychology, could quickly become a source of serious and damaging dissension. There was also a very real danger in the mere presence of an unwieldy mob at Massabielle. The circular space in front of the grotto was small. Spectators who did not arrive in time to find room there mounted on the large stones rising above the Gave or climbed the trees overhanging the hollow. A false step on the slippery surface of the stones would have meant a precipitate plunge into the river; the breaking of a branch under too much weight would have meant a swift drop into space. It seemed to the authorities that such accidents had so far been averted by good luck rather than by good management. In the interest of common prudence it was thought best not to trust too much to chance. All were agreed that though they must proceed cautiously in order not to rouse the resentment of the credulous crowd, they must stifle the agitation at its source. Since the little girl herself was responsible for it, she must be forbidden to go to the grotto and the prohibition must be enforced. The *Procureur Imperial*, Monsieur Dutour, who was a man of many fine qualities but some strong prejudices, accordingly summoned Bernadette before him.

"My child," he said, speaking not unkindly at first, "you are causing a good deal of talk. Do you intend to continue your visits to the grotto?"

"Yes, sir. I have made a promise to the Lady, and I shall continue going there for another twelve days."

"But my poor child, your Lady doesn't exist; she is a purely imaginary being."

"I thought so, too, when I saw her for the first time, and I rubbed my eyes, but now I know for certain that I am not mistaken."

"How do you know that?"

"Because I have seen her many times. I saw her only this morning. Moreover, she talks with me."

"The Hospice Sisters to whom you go to school would not tell a lie, yet they tell you that you are under a delusion."

37

"If the Sisters of the Hospice saw as I do, they would believe as I do."

"Take care. Before we have done we shall perhaps discover some secrets which will explain your obstinacy. It is already said that you and your parents have received presents privately."

"We receive nothing from anyone."

"But yesterday you went to Madame Millet, and there you had some sweets given you."

"Quite true; Madame Millet made me take a glass of water and sugar for my asthma, but that was all."

"However that may be, your conduct at the grotto is a veritable scandal. You are disturbing the town and all this must be stopped. Will you promise me not to return to Massabielle?"

"Sir, I cannot promise you that."

"Is that your final word?"

"Yes, sir."

"Go away then. . . . I shall think over what is to be done."

Such was the tenor of their talk as Monsieur Dutour repeated it later at his club to a group of his friends, Monsieur Estrade among them, laughing over his own setback as he did so. Monsieur Jacomet, the Chief of Police, was not inclined to treat the matter so lightly. Later the same afternoon he went to the Place du Porche, where he had been led to expect he would find Bernadette coming from Vespers. He had not been misinformed. The court usher pointed her out to his chief as she walked quietly along beside her Aunt Lucille, and Monsieur Jacomet approached her and asked her to come to his office.

She followed him without objection. Her aunt went

off to tell the family what had happened, and some little friends, seeing her alone with the officer of the law, called out to her with the taunting cruelty of the young that they supposed she was being led away to prison. She called back that she was not afraid and that there was no reason why she should be as she had done nothing wrong.

She certainly did not appear to be afraid when Monsieur Estrade, availing himself of a neighbor's privilege, went down to the Police Commissioner's apartment to see for himself exactly what was happening. "The child before me, whom I saw for the first time, appeared to be ten or eleven years of age, but she was really fourteen," he wrote afterward. "Her face was fresh and round, her gaze was very sweet and very simple. The tone of her voice, though somewhat loud, was sympathetic. I did not notice her asthma. In a very natural attitude she kept her hands crossed upon her knees and her head slightly bent forward over her chest. She was wearing a white cloak, and her other garments though simple were clean and neat. A table with a desk upon it separated her from the Commissioner.

"When I came in Monsieur Jacomet had just finished settling himself in his seat and was placing in front of him a sheet of blank paper and a pencil. Then he turned to the child and said to her in his most insidiously kind manner:

" 'I expect you know why I have summoned you here. People have told me of all the beautiful things you have seen at Massabielle and I am so interested that I want to hear all about it. Would you mind telling Monsieur Estrade and me how you first met the Lady of the Grotto?'

" 'Not at all, sir.'

39

" 'Your name is Bernadette, isn't it?'

" 'Yes, sir. Bernadette.'

" 'What is your surname?'

"The child considered for a moment, as if she did not quite understand. Then she replied, 'Bernadette Soubirous.'

" 'How old are you?'

" 'Fourteen.'

" 'You're quite sure?' said the Commissioner, smiling, as if to ask whether she was not exaggerating.

" 'Yes, sir, I am quite sure. I've turned fourteen.'

" 'What do you do in the house?'

" 'Nothing very much, sir. Since my return from Bartrès I have been going to school to learn the catechism; after school I look after my brothers and sister, who are younger than I.'

" 'So you lived at Bartrès? What did you do there?'

" 'I spent several months at my foster mother's house; she gave me a little flock of sheep and lambs to look after.'

"The Commissioner in a friendly tone asked a few more questions of the child. When he thought he had secured her confidence, he said to her, 'Now let us come to what we want you to tell us, namely, the scene under the rock at Massabielle which has made so strong an impression upon you. Take as long as you like in telling us about it.'

"Bernadette . . . entered into all the details of age, costume, face, relating to the Lady, and that with such convinced simplicity that one could not for a moment doubt her sincerity. While she spoke, the Commissioner wrote rapidly upon his paper. Then he raised his head.

40

THE SHEEP-FOLD ON THE PASTURE NEAR BARTRES

THE BIRTHPLACE OF BERNADETTE SOUBIROUS

" 'What you tell us is very interesting, but who is this Lady who has so infatuated you? Do you know her?'

" 'I do not know her,' answered the child with a touching simplicity.

" 'You say she is beautiful. How beautiful is she?'

" 'Oh, sir, she is more beautiful than any lady I have ever met.'

" 'But not more beautiful than Madame N—— or Madame N——?' Here the Commissioner mentioned the names of the most beautiful ladies at Lourdes.

" 'They can't be compared with her.'

" 'Does this Lady move and speak, or does she remain in her place like a statue in a church?'

" 'Oh, she moves and smiles and speaks like you; among other things she has asked me to be so kind as to return to the grotto during the next fifteen days.'

" 'What did you say?'

" 'I have promised that I will return.'

" 'What do your parents say about these things?'

" 'At first, they said they were illusions—'

"Seizing upon this word as it passed her lips, the Commissioner interrupted her:

" 'Yes, my child, your parents are right, and the things which you think you hear and see exist only in your imagination.'

" 'Others have said so to me, but I am sure that I am not mistaken.'

" 'Listen. If the Lady of the rock was a person like other persons, everyone would be able to see her and hear her. How is it that this is not so?'

" 'I cannot explain these things to you, sir. What I can positively affirm is that the Lady is real and living.'

41

" 'Since you hold to it, I have no reason to prevent your believing in the existence of your pretended Lady. However, as the prefect or some other authority will probably require of me a report on this subject, let us see if I have got all your answers down correctly.'

"Here the Commissioner took his paper of notes and began a war of traps. He tried to make Bernadette contradict herself.

" 'You said that the Lady was aged about nineteen or twenty?'

" 'No, I said sixteen or seventeen.'

" 'That she was dressed in a blue robe with a white girdle?'

" 'Just the opposite, sir; you should have put a white robe with a blue girdle.'

" 'That her hair fell down behind?'

" 'You have misunderstood me; it is the veil which fell down behind.'

"And so Bernadette corrected, without boldness but also without timidity, all the mistakes which the Commissioner had introduced into her story on purpose. Monsieur Jacomet understood that nothing was to be gained in this way, so he changed his tactics. Speaking to her seriously and somewhat ironically, he said:

" 'My dear Bernadette, I wished to let you go on to the end of your tale but I ought to let you know that I was familiar with the story of your pretended visions before. This story is pure invention and I know who is responsible for it.'

"The young girl raised her astonished eyes to the man in front of her and replied, 'I don't understand you, sir.'

" 'I will be more explicit. Is there not someone who

has secretly told you to say that the Virgin appeared to you at Massabielle, and that by saying this you will not only pass for a saint but also obtain great favor from the Virgin? Be careful in your answer, for I know more about this matter than you think.'

" 'No one, sir, has suggested to me the things of which you speak.'

" 'I know the whole state of the case but I don't want to cause a scandal or seek a quarrel. I don't demand any confession from you, but you must give me one simple promise. Will you assure me that you will not go again to the grotto?'

" 'Sir, I have promised the Lady to return there.'

" 'Oh, indeed,' said the Commissioner, rising from his seat and feigning anger, 'so, you imagine that we are always going to listen good-naturedly to your fairy tales and give way to your obstinacy? If you do not instantly promise me not to return to Massabielle I will send for the gendarmes and have you put in prison.'

"Bernadette remained immovable.

"I now left my place and came up to the child.

" 'My child, don't be obstinate. Do what Monsieur Jacomet asks you; if not, you know what to expect.'

"Bernadette understood that I had no authority to interfere and she gave me no answer. Meanwhile the door of the pretorium opened and a workingman timidly put in his head.

" 'What do you want?' the Commissioner asked.

" 'I am the child's father,' the man replied, pointing to Bernadette.

" 'Ah! You are Monsieur Soubirous. I am glad you have come, for I was just about to send for you. You

43

know the game your daughter has been playing for some days. Put up to do it no doubt by some mischievous old woman of the district, she pretends to be inspired and gives herself up to tricks which are turning the heads of imbeciles. This comedy must end, for it constitutes a real danger to the peace of the town. I warn you that if you have not enough authority to keep your child at home, I shall have enough to cause her to be shut up elsewhere.'

" 'Oh, sir, please let me speak frankly. For myself, I have no doubt that the child is sincere in the story which she tells, but is she mistaken? That is what puzzles us. I confess to you that my wife and I are worn out with importunities. I am glad to have your orders as an excuse for shutting out the public. As to Bernadette, we will see that she does not go near Massabielle any more.' "

François and Louise Soubirous both meant to see to it. So did the Police Commissioner. The next day when Bernadette started to school with her little basket on her arm, it was with the stern injunction that she was to look neither to the right nor to the left. She obeyed punctiliously in the morning; but in the afternoon, when she reached the point where the road runs from the Pont des Ruisseaux to the Hospice, she wavered. Later on she insisted that "an invisible barrier" prevented her from going forward, and she was almost tempted to go home. At the same time, the "still small voice within her" reminded her that she was breaking the promise which she had made to the Beautiful Lady. After several moments of hesitation, she turned and took an indirect path to Massabielle.

At this time the police barracks was situated on the Route de Tarbes, not far from the point where the child

44

had stopped; and two gendarmes, mindful of their chief's orders, who had been watching her attentively from the window, lost no time in following her. When they caught up with her, they asked her where she was going. She flung back her answer over her shoulder.

"To the grotto," she said, without pausing or turning.

They did not try to stop her, but continued to follow her, marching stiffly behind her. The usual crowd collected as she went by, the bristling gendarmes striding in her wake. The child was apparently oblivious of any commotion or any cause for it. When she reached "her own place" she knelt down quietly. The gendarmes came to a halt behind her and stood at attention. As she rose from her knees, they sprang forward, commanding her to tell them what she had seen.

"Nothing at all," she answered.(12)

It must have been a moment of supreme humiliation. She had disobeyed her parents, she had defied the Police Commissioner, she had disregarded the gendarmes. She had quailed, but she had persevered. And at the end of the hard road, instead of winning the reward which she so confidently sought, she had been turned empty handed from the holy place. There had been no golden light, no celestial vision, no close communion. The crowd, quick to sense her chagrin, had already begun to taunt her with the fickleness of its kind.

"The Beautiful Lady must be afraid of the police!" it jeered. "She is wise enough to know that if that fox Jacomet is mixed up in this she had better decamp! She has left her rock and her rosebush and found a safer place!"

The raucous cries followed the little girl as she picked

45

her weary way home. If she had been a fraud, they would certainly have frightened her away for all times. The greatest proof of her sincerity lies in the fact that two days later she went sturdily back to the grotto.(13) She had her just recompense. She was entrusted by the Beautiful Lady with three secrets. This much she told. But she never told any more.

⚜ FIVE ⚜

THE THREE secrets were not the first mark of special favor which the little girl had been granted. When Bernadette left the grotto after her fifth visit(14) she said that the Beautiful Lady had taught her, word for word, a prayer which was for her alone. She never told the text, though all the rest of her life she recited this prayer every day. But one by one she did disclose other revelations. At one of the first apparitions, she had been told by the Beautiful Lady that she should always present herself carrying a lighted candle, which afterward she should take home with her: a candle of the Children of Mary, a candle that had been blessed. On a later occasion, the Beautiful Lady told her to leave the candle behind her. She propped it up, with stones, near the great rock; there it burnt itself out. Her gesture was imitated, and from that day to this, there have always been candles burning in the grotto.(15)

Then there was the thrice-repeated warning of "Penitence,"(16) the injunction to "pray for sinners,"(17) and to "kiss the ground in behalf of sinners."(18) Bernadette had quickly bent over and touched the soil with her lips when this command came. It had not been hard to under-

47

stand, and everyone around her had been spontaneously moved to do the same. But meanwhile another order had proved far more mysterious: "Go drink from the fountain and bathe in it!"(19)

No spring had ever been seen at Massabielle. Bernadette did not know what to do. She rose from her knees, looked around her and finally turned to the left. Then, tentatively, she began to scrape away at the gravel. After a moment a small pool appeared from which water slowly bubbled up. The little girl made a cup of her hands and drank from it three times; then, slowly and seriously, she washed her face. The next day a trickle of water was already dripping down from the place she had scraped; the day after, it had become a slender stream. It was easy enough to say—and of course this was said—that a spring must have always existed at Massabielle but no one had ever noticed it before. The fact still remained that it was Bernadette who had discovered it and that something supernatural had impelled her to discover it.

The next commands that came from the Beautiful Lady were even more baffling and bewildering. The first of these was that Bernadette should tell the clergy to build a chapel at this place;(20) the second that people should form processionals to visit it.(21)

The parish priest of Lourdes, Abbé Peyramale, had taken no apparent notice of the extraordinary events at the grotto, though he had been giving serious thought to them. He was a large, imposing man with a severe face, a penetrating glance and a brusque manner. Bernadette was terribly afraid of him. But as she thought herself in duty bound to tell him about the chapel, she mustered all her courage and set out to call on him. He hardly knew her by sight; indeed, he had seen her only once, in the midst of the large catechism class at the Hospice, when she answered to her name in the roll call. Therefore, as the unfamiliar figure of a little girl appeared at the gate of his courtyard seeking admission while he was tranquilly pacing up and down his garden path busy with his breviary, he frowned as he closed his book and asked the child in a cold voice who she was and what she wanted.

"I am Bernadette Soubirous," the little girl said timidly, feeling more frightened than ever.

"Oh, you are, are you? I have been hearing some very strange stories about you. Follow me."

He turned stiffly and led the way into the presbytery. Bernadette followed him with a beating heart. When they were inside he turned again and confronted her sternly.

"What do you want?" he asked, for the second time.

Bernadette blushed furiously. It was much harder, even, than she had supposed beforehand it would be. But she held her ground.

"Please, Monsieur le Curé," she said, trying to keep her voice under control, "the Lady of the Grotto has ordered me to tell the clergy that she wishes to have a chapel built at Massabielle. That is why I have come."

"But who is this Lady of whom you speak?"

"She is a very beautiful Lady who appeared to me on the Massabielle rock."

"Well, but *who* is this Lady? Is she from Lourdes? Do you know her?"

"She is not from Lourdes and I do not know her."

49

"And you undertake to carry such a message as the one you have just given me from a person whom you don't know?"

"Oh, Monsieur le Curé, the Lady who sends me is not like other ladies."

"What do you mean?"

"I mean that she is as beautiful as they are in heaven, I should think."

"And have you never asked this Lady her name?"

"Yes, but when I ask her she bows her head slightly, smiles and gives me no answer."

"Is she then dumb?"

"No, because she talks to me every day. If she were dumb she would not have been able to tell me to come to you."

"Tell me how you came to meet her."

Slightly encouraged, Bernadette told the story of the first apparition. When she had finished, the priest said, "Go on and tell me what happened on the days following." The child gave him a detailed account of all that she had seen and heard at the grotto up to that time.

While she was speaking the Curé motioned Bernadette to a seat and sat down himself. He looked at her fixedly and did not lose one word of what she said. Her sincerity convinced him that she was telling the truth as she understood it, and, moreover, he realized that it would be difficult for an unlettered little peasant to invent instructions of the type she was outlining. He concealed his impressions, however, questioning her as at the beginning of their interview in a gruff tone of voice.

"And you say that the Lady who appeared to you

ordered you to say to the priests that she wished to have a chapel at Massabielle?"

"Yes, Monsieur le Curé."

"But don't you see that this Lady was laughing at you and making you ridiculous? If a lady in the town had told you to take such a message, would you have obeyed her?"

"But there is a great difference between the ladies in the town and the Lady whom I have seen."

"I should think there *is* a difference! You imagine that a woman who has no name and comes from nowhere, who takes up her abode on a rock and has bare feet, deserves to be taken seriously? My child, there is one thing I do fear, and that is that you are the victim of an illusion."

Bernadette hung her head and gave no answer. There was a moment's silence during which the Curé rose from his seat and began to pace up and down the room. He came back, stopped in front of Bernadette and said to her:

"Tell the Lady who has sent you that the Curé of Lourdes is not in the habit of dealing with people whom he does not know; say that before everything else he demands to know her name, and that moreover she must prove that this name belongs to her. If this Lady has the right to a chapel she will understand the meaning of my words; if she does not understand, tell her that she need not trouble to send me any more messages."

Bernadette looked quietly up at the Curé, made a quick little curtsy and went away. The good pastor watched her to the gate, and when she was out of sight he could not refrain from saying to himself, "This is most certainly a child of divine providence."

Unfortunately she was not aware of what a good impression she had created; and having been so severely treated when she transmitted the first mysterious message, she was doubly afraid to return with the second one. But by slow degrees she again screwed up her courage, and this time she persuaded her Aunt Basile to go with her and keep her countenance. The Curé gave them a cold welcome. Indeed, he commiserated with Bernadette's aunt on being related to a child who had thrown the city into a state of disorder, adding that "Lourdes was lost because of her."(22) And his face darkened when the little girl told him that the Beautiful Lady had repeated her wish to have a chapel built at Massabielle and that this time she had added, "I want people to come here in processions."

"This is a fitting climax to all your stories," he said sternly. "Either you are lying or the Lady who speaks to you is only a fraud. Why does she want a procession? Doubtless to make unbelievers laugh and to turn religion into ridicule. The trap is not very cleverly laid. You can tell her from me that she knows very little about the powers and responsibilities of the clergy. If she were really what she pretends to be she would know that I am not qualified to take the initiative in such a matter. It is to the Bishop of Tarbes, not to me, that she ought to have sent you."

"But, sir," interrupted Bernadette timidly, "the Lady did not tell me that she wanted a procession to the grotto *immediately;* she only said, 'I want people to come here in processions,' and if I understood her rightly she was speaking of the future and not of the present."

The Curé stopped short at this remark and cast a look

of searching scrutiny upon the child. What was the meaning of this explanation given by Bernadette of the message? Was the Curé really in the presence of a cunning actress who was throwing dust in his eyes by her airs of innocence? Abbé Peyramale felt all his old prejudices revive once more.

"It is high time for me to get out of the imbroglio in which the Lady and you seek to entangle me," he said at last. "Tell her that with the Curé of Lourdes she must speak clearly and concisely. She wants a chapel, she wants a procession. What title has she to these honors which she claims? Who is she? Where does she come from and what has she done to deserve our homage? Don't let us beat about. If your Lady is the one your messages suggest, I will show her a means of obtaining recognition and giving authority to these messages. You tell me she stands in the grotto, above a rosebush. Well, ask her from me to make the bush in question burst into flower one day suddenly in the presence of the assembled multitude. The morning when you come to tell me that this phenomenon has taken place I will believe your word and I promise to go with you to Massabielle."

❀ SIX ❀

THE Curé of Lourdes was not the only person who was eager to learn the name of the Beautiful Lady. Public curiosity concerning it had continued to swell. Even the Parisian press had begun to discuss the subject. The crowds at the grotto were no longer limited to the inhabitants of Lourdes. Strangers were coming there from far and wide.

On the third of March the Mayor of Lourdes addressed a petition to the commandant of the fort, asking for a military guard to supplement the police force. The famous "fortnight" would be up the next day. He was sure that multitudes would arrive in the expectation of some special revelation. He did not feel that he could cope with the situation unaided.

The commandant responded handsomely. At break of dawn the entire garrison reported, in full dress, at the Mayor's office. The soldiers were soon stationed at intervals along the road to Massabielle, rifles in hand. In addition, several brigades of gendarmes, some of them mounted, who had been brought in from outside, were detailed to clear the roads so that the little shepherdess

54

might have a free passage. The local brigade was drawn up beneath the arcade of the grotto like a guard of honor. The Mayor, the Deputy Mayor and the Police Commissioner, all wearing their insignia of office, circulated through the immense crowd with an air of mingled importance and conviviality. About twenty thousand persons had forgathered, for whom they were responsible, and they wished to make an impressive show of both hospitality and authority. It was a great day for Lourdes.

Bernadette tried to leave *Le Cachot* as quietly as possible. But she had hardly crossed the threshold when a murmur arose which swelled into a sort of song: "Bernadette is coming, Bernadette is coming." Waves of magnetic force seemed released as she went along. She was not tracked by policemen this time. Instead, they marched ahead of her with drawn swords, as if she had been a great personage for whom they must clear the path. The excited strangers along the line strained their eyes and craned their necks to have a good look at her. All they saw was a little peasant girl with a colored kerchief over her dark hair and a full cloak falling around her, who looked like a shepherdess and walked tranquilly along, as if she were guarding her sheep on the hillside pasture. Only once did she give a sign of noticing anyone near her. That was when a blind girl, standing close to the grotto, suddenly burst out crying. Bernadette stopped and, putting her arms around the child, kissed her and comforted her.

It was after she had knelt down that the strangers searching for a remarkable spectacle were impressed and awed. They had heard much about the ethereal beauty with which the little girl became mysteriously transfigured. Now they saw it for themselves. This beauty was not confined to her illumined face. It was also revealed in her posture and in her prayer. Every movement she made was full of grace, from the gesture with which she first bent her head to the one with which she bowed as the vision vanished. The manner in which she made the sign of the cross and held her rosary had supreme dignity. The shepherdess was submerged. A queen, or an abbess, might well have copied her carriage.

This revelation was all that the multitudes had anticipated—and more. But there was no other. When Bernadette rose from her knees, the clamoring crowd came as close to her as the *gendarmerie* would permit, plying her with questions. She had almost nothing to say. Yes, she had seen the Beautiful Lady as usual. Yes, the Lady had smiled. No, she had not said good-by. Yes, Bernadette meant to keep on coming to the grotto. No, she was not sure whether the Lady would do so also, now that the "fortnight" was over. There was nothing more to say—

The reaction from tensity was not immediate. As she turned to leave the grotto, still preceded by the police, the masses surged around her. Some of them even braved the bared bayonets in order to touch her. But presently the exaltation passed. What, after all, had happened? Nothing that had been most eagerly awaited. The rosebush had not flowered, the vision had not been made manifest. The name of the Beautiful Lady was still undisclosed. Murmuring again, the multitudes dispersed and went to their own homes. The soldiers put up their swords and formed no more guards of honor. The Mayor, the Deputy Mayor and the Police Commissioner laid aside

BERNADETTE IN HER PEASANT DRESS

Dicté du 1er Novembre 1865°

Saint-Pierre de Rome.

Ce monument entrepris par le génie... est un des plus... lorsque l'on connaîtra que...

Rien ne saurait exprimer ce ravissement sublime qui saisit l'âme, lorsqu'on entre pour la première fois dans cette Église, lorsque one se trouve sur ce pavé de marbres par-mis des piliers énormes, de vastes colonnes de Bronze, à la place de tous ces tableaux, de toutes les statues, de tous ces Marbres, de tout ce... de toutes ces Dames, enfin dans ce... immense, infinie, à laquelle ce... de marbre, ce bronze, ce... ce... donne tant de grandeur, de magnificence, de... !

their scarves and resumed their regular routine. Only a faithful few, who had already raised a rustic altar at Massabielle, continued to go there to pray. Bernadette herself retreated from the public gaze.

She did so gratefully. She had never sought it, never desired it. She was thankful to think that all the storm and stress which had raged around her were over, that she could live again the ordered life that she liked. She went back and forth to school. She played with her friends. She gathered fagots. She took care of her little brothers. Only when all this was done did she go to the grotto, late in the afternoon as dusk began to fall, choosing circuitous ways, half hidden by her dark cloak.

Still, there were some days when there was no school. There were Sundays, of course, and feast days. Indeed, a great feast day was approaching: the Festival of the Annunciation, which falls on the twenty-fifth of March— the anniversary of the Angel Gabriel's visit to Mary of Nazareth, when the "Word was made Man."

Offices as well as schools were closed on that day. And so it came about that Monsieur Estrade, the Collector of *Contributions Indirectes,* was sitting restfully at home with his sister when the door of their apartment was flung open and Bernadette burst in upon them.

She had been back to the grotto, in the morning this time, because she did not have to go to the Hospice, and the Beautiful Lady was already there when she reached it! The recess was "aglow with glory"! And after she had saluted the vision and recited her rosary, Bernadette had suddenly felt her heart grow bold, bolder than it had ever been before. She begged the Beautiful Lady, as she had done before, to reveal her name. Only this time, when she did not receive an immediate reply, she pressed for it. She asked three times. The third time she clasped her hands as she made the request and she made it urgently. And then, at last, the long-awaited answer had come.

"Que soy era Immaculada Conceptión."

"What does it mean?" the child cried, looking trustfully at Mademoiselle Estrade for enlightenment. "What does concep-tión mean?"

She could not even pronounce the word correctly. She had heard it used before, vaguely, in connection with the Mother of God. But no one had ever told her what it meant and she had never asked. At that time, nearly a century ago, the doctrine of the Immaculate Conception had only recently (1854) been defined by Pius IX as an article of Faith. Bernadette's joy was mingled with perplexity. She turned to her trusted friends for enlightenment.

But if she herself was uncomprehending, there were hundreds of others who were not. The excitement concerning the visions, dormant for three weeks, was instantly awake and crying again. Friends meeting on the street fell on each other's necks with mutual felicitations, as if they were responsible for the great events. Strangers began to pour into town once more. The authorities resumed their activities. The Mayor and the Public Commissioner of Lourdes, feeling that the time had come to consult a high official, wrote to the Prefect of Tarbes, Baron Massy, who was responsible for the entire department. Considerably annoyed, he gave instructions that the little girl should be examined by three responsible doctors, to see whether she should not be consigned to an asylum.

58

The examination took place in the parlor at the Hospice of which the Sisters were so proud, in the presence of the Mother Superior. Encompassed by the square piano, the marble mantel and the towering secretary, the physicians sat in the red velvet armchairs and questioned the little girl. Dr. Dozous was not among them. In spite of his high standing, he had been set aside as prejudiced because of what he had already seen and said. But his colleagues, after trying in vain to trip Bernadette up, abandoned the attempt in despair. They reported that while it was possible she might have been the victim of an optical illusion, she was certainly sane of mind and sound of body. They thought that in the course of normal events she would probably forget all about the grotto. In their opinion, the sooner she was allowed to resume her regular routine, the better it would be for all concerned.

Baron Massy, upon reading this report, was increasingly annoyed, and a letter which he received shortly afterward from the Mayor augmented his bad temper still further. He read it fumingly:

"The crowd at the grotto continues as large as ever and Eastertide, in which we now are, adds to it considerably. The great majority of visitors go for reasons of piety and pray to God with much fervor. I presume that this crowd will decrease after the festivals.

"So long as public tranquillity reigns and order is not disturbed, I suppose there is nothing to be done. If you think otherwise, please give me fresh instructions and I will follow them exactly."(23)

He did not give fresh instructions immediately, but Eastertide brought with it a fresh phenomenon, and with

59

it the expected increase in crowds. On the seventh of April, as Bernadette knelt in the grotto, she held in her left hand the lighted candle which, in accordance with the Beautiful Lady's instructions, she now never failed to bring with her. During her ecstasy, she made an unconscious movement with her right hand. Her fingers passed over the candle and enveloped the flame; its point appeared above the hollow formed by her hand; its brilliance blazed through the translucency of her flesh. The crowd cried out in horror; a frightful accident seemed both imminent and inevitable. But Bernadette remained immovable and unscathed; it was fully fifteen minutes before her expression of rapture changed, and then her face resumed its accustomed look of tranquillity, untouched by pain. Her fingers were unscorched. It was only when Dr. Dozous, who had again been present, decided to make a crucial experiment that she gave any sign of shock. When he took a lighted candle himself, and, unperceived by her, brought it brusquely into contact with her hand, she recoiled with a cry. "You are burning me!" she exclaimed reproachfully.

The effect of all this was overwhelming. Before long Baron Massy received another letter saying the crowds were increasing instead of diminishing, and still another reminding him that no place of public worship—such as the grotto was rapidly becoming—could be set up without the permission of both the civil and ecclesiastical authorities; then he decided to wait upon the Bishop of Tarbes, Monseigneur Laurence, who was a most remarkable man. The Bishop himself had sprung from surroundings almost as humble as Bernadette's and had buoyantly risen above them. At the age of twenty-one he

60

had hardly been able to read and write; at the age of thirty-one he had been ordained; at the age of fifty-five he "carried his episcopal crosier where as a boy he had borne his shepherd's crook." He was shrewd, thoughtful and temperate. He had no idea of committing himself to hasty action on the subject which so disturbed the Prefect, and he informed that functionary to this effect. Their conversation is meticulously recorded by Estrade.

The Bishop began by telling the Prefect that he did not share the latter's anxiety and that he could not commit himself to hasty action. "If the appearances at the grotto were unmistakably true or unmistakably false my duty would be easy," he said, "and I should let everyone know my opinion in the matter. But in the difficult conditions of the present problem, the Bishop's duty is to suspend judgment and to wait until Providence has plainly revealed the truth. This will be my line of conduct in the matter of Massabielle, and if you like, you have my authority to inform the Minister of Public Worship of my decision."

"Your silence, Monseigneur, may become a danger to the public peace."

"That is not my opinion. People pray at the grotto and prayer is never a danger."

"But if some people pray at the grotto, others mock."

"You are misinformed. I can assure you that the behavior of those at the grotto is most reverent," the Bishop said. "In conclusion," he added, "do not let us waste our time in argument but let us make our positions clear. You, I have no doubt, reduce the fact of Lourdes to the simple proportions of an administrative difficulty and you are in haste to put an end to it. I on the other hand see in the matter a question of a much higher order, and this question I am convinced will demand from me long and continued thought. Our views are so divergent that we are far from an agreement."

"Allow me to remark, Monseigneur, that a veritable center of public worship has been established at the grotto of Massabielle, and that in contempt of the law. The administration cannot allow at Lourdes what it forbids elsewhere."

"Your scruples in this matter are no concern of mine. However, before you set to work, I should advise you to think your plans over carefully."

"I, like you, Monseigneur, have rules to follow and duties to fulfill. I do not intend to neglect my responsibilities."

The parting between the Prelate and the Prefect is described as having been "stiff," which is easy to believe. Shortly afterward they had an equally decided difference of opinion about some Church property; and from then on their relations continued strained. But the next time the Prefect made an official visit to Lourdes, he took matters into his own hands; over the protests, some mute and some voiced, of the local authorities, he ordered the rustic altar dismantled and the grotto closed. There was considerable consternation and some demonstration. But eventually these died down. To all appearances, the question of the apparitions was closed, too.

Bernadette herself would have been the last to try to keep it open. There had been no apparition since Easter-time; and in May a distant relative, the wife of a Civil Guard at Lourdes, took her Cauterets, in the hope that the mineral springs there would improve her health, about which the good woman felt much concerned. She spent two calm and restful weeks there, shielded from public curiosity and removed from controversial agitation. But aside from this interval Bernadette had no respite, and she was finding that fame, no less than obscurity, has its disadvantages. *Le Cachot* was never free from intruders. They came to talk endlessly, to expostulate, to exclaim, to say the same thing over and over themselves, and to ask the same questions. Bernadette had never been voluble; their endless chitchat wearied and distressed her. Moreover, these chatterers asked all kinds of favors as well as all kinds of questions, and they brought with them all sorts of bribes. Though, of course, the Soubirous had never heard the classic declaration "*Timeo Danaos et dona ferentes,*" they nevertheless harbored the same feeling. Destitute as they still were, they refused everything that was offered them, even to the baskets of simple provender brought into them by their old friends in the country. It was hard when they were hungry. But too many strings were attached to most of the prize packages dangled before their eyes. François Soubirous stood in deadly fear of being led into a trap and imprisoned for some crime he had not actually committed; he had already had one such experience. Louise possessed the shrinking of her kind from anything that could be called queer. The younger children alone were tempted by *sous* and sweetmeats. Bernadette saw to it that these were all returned. She was determined that no one should tarnish the pure gold of her vision.

Although an aeon had seemingly elapsed since her departure from Bartrès, it was actually less than six months. She still looked like a shepherdess, carrying her head slightly bent forward when she walked and holding her hands tranquilly folded in her lap when she sat down. She still went back and forth to the Hospice, carrying over her arm the little basket which contained the stockings she was knitting, the bit of black bread which was her *gouter,* and the well-worn primer from which she was learning to read. At recess, she romped with her schoolmates in the galleried garden, and joined in all their games. During catechism, she behaved much as they did; sometimes she was attentive and sometimes she was abstracted. But she continued to prepare for the sacraments which she had come back to Lourdes on purpose to receive. If all her preparations were not visible to her preceptors and her fellow pupils, there is no doubt that they were understood Elsewhere.

She made her First Communion the third of June, wearing the traditional costume which little girls assume in France for this rite—the long white dress, the flowing veil, the snowy ornaments. On this one occasion, she had not declined to accept a gift, for otherwise she could not have gone to the altar suitably clad, and her happy benefactor had not failed to consider the beautiful and the becoming. Bernadette's soft dress was daintily stitched, her sheer veil embroidered. She was not shamed before her companions who, in a worldly sense, were more fortunate than she.

The habit of frequent Communion, even among the devout, was not nearly as general a century ago as it is now. But like most human beings mystically endowed, Bernadette felt the constant urge to repeat the experience for which she had begun to long amid the silences of her pastureland. By the middle of July she had already sought the satisfaction of it several times, and on the Feast of Our Lady of Carmel, which falls on the sixteenth of that month, the sense of beatitude which enfolded her as she left the altar rail abode with her through the day. As evening approached, this seemed to take on a new significance; she felt impelled to go where she could gaze toward the grotto. She knew that she could not enter it freely, to pray there. It was bare now, and barricaded, by the order of the Prefect. But at least she could look toward it, lovingly, from the farther side of the Gave. She asked her Aunt Basile, who had so often accompanied her willingly in the past, to go with her, and they set out by a meadow road which skirted the right of the river.

When they reached a stopping place, they found that they were not alone. Two or three small groups of humble women were kneeling in the grass, with their faces turned toward the grotto. The Prefect had possessed the power to burn their altar and bar them from the place which they held holy. But he had not been able to change their hearts or shake their faith. When they saw Bernadette coming, they moved together, as by common accord, and made a semicircle around her, mingling their prayers with hers. And almost instantly they knew that she had seen what she sought. The look which they knew so well came into her face: it shone with reflected radiance. The sun sank down behind the trees and from the mountaintops the coolness of evening descended. The same stillness which the shepherdess had found in the fields enfolded them all.

It was a supreme moment, marking the end of one era and the beginning of another. Bernadette never saw the Beautiful Lady again.

✸ SEVEN ✸

I⊤ was customary for little girls of Bernadette's station to stop their schooling after they had made their First Communion The Sisters at the Hospice saw no reason for making an exception to this rule, and Bernadette no longer went back and forth, carrying her little basket over her arm. She remained all the time with her family.

This arrangement did not work out very well. The end of the apparitions had not been the end of the excitement. The opposition of the authorities had rekindled a flame instead of killing it. Strangers kept on coming to Lourdes. Miracles were attributed to the spring at the grotto. Bernadette was the object of continued curiosity, and there was no way of protecting her from the importunities of her visitors. She was almost killed with mistaken kindness. The town officials conferred with the Sisters, and as a result of this conference she was asked to return to the Hospice, not as a day pupil but as a *pensionnaire*. She gratefully accepted.

She was not put into the dormitory with the rest of the girls, but given a bright, sunny room all her own. She also had her own special place in the dining room. Although the ostensible reason for her entry at the Hospice was her health—her asthma had become more and more troublesome and she did need care and nourishment—she was never placed among the rest of the ailing and needy poor for whom the Sisters cared. She was the cherished child of a group of childless women. To some observers, they seemed to take her presence for granted. To others, it appeared as if they underestimated her worth and relegated her to menial tasks in order to humiliate her, even neglecting to praise her for accomplishing them well. As a matter of fact, this was the sort of task she preferred, and praise, like publicity, disturbed her. It was always her instinct to remain in the background.

When pilgrims of special distinction came to Lourdes, she was led into the formidable parlor to talk with them. Curiosity seekers were not permitted to harass her in and out of season, as they had while she was still at home. Nevertheless, she continued to find these visits a trial. Frequently she was found crying on the threshold of the parlor, and it took time for her to collect herself. But inside she showed the same calmness which she had always displayed. If she was permitted to follow her own inclinations, she talked about simple things which were natural to her, like crops and harvests. The Sous Prefect's wife, who had looked forward with excitement to seeing her, could recall nothing remarkable about the interview afterward; Bernadette had asked her whether there were many walnuts that year and whether they were good. This was about all she had said. When she was pressed to give a recital of the apparitions, she did so, but no one could shake her story or her composure. Once she was

67

haughtily informed that the Beautiful Lady's girdle could not possibly have been pale blue, since this color was contrary to certain ritualistic rulings. "I know nothing about those. I only know that the belt was blue," she replied imperturbably. On another occasion, a petulant lady exclaimed that she could not be expected to believe such a phantasy as Bernadette had woven. "I did not ask you to believe it, I only told you what I had seen," Bernadette answered.

The members of the commission appointed by the Bishop for purposes of investigation also put pointed questions to her, and more than once were not only answered but routed. The President of this commission, for instance, spoke to her severely about the blade of grass she has nibbled, after she had poked about in the ground and released the first muddy bubbles which were so soon followed by a rush of limpid water. "How could you do such a thing?" he said rebukingly. "Don't you know that only animals eat raw green stuff?" She smiled pleasantly. "Oh, Monsieur l'Abbé, surely you are mistaken," she retorted without a moment's hesitation. "Why, we eat salad every day!"

The unique character of the favors which had been shown her was exploited by others, but never by her. "So you are the only person who has ever seen this vision?" still another visitor, who had penetrated to her presence, inquired rapturously. "I don't know for certain. I have heard it said that the Mayor's serving maid saw it, too," was the almost casual rejoinder. Her own schoolmates, who, like the nuns, were used to her, sometimes tried to tease her by saying, "So you have really seen the Blessed Virgin, Bernadette?" Other young girls coming from a distance put the same question, but with awe and admiration. Her answer was the same in both cases. "I never said I saw the Blessed Virgin. I said I saw a Beautiful Lady."

The Sisters took her occasionally to the grotto. She said that those were her "most beautiful days." But she never begged to be taken there. It is probable that she went, in spirit, every day by herself. She continued to recite her rosary with unfailing regularity. Even at night she kept it entwined between her fingers. She also received Communion, gladly and frequently, and it was due to her constancy in this respect that the doubts which Abbé Peyramale had continued to entertain were finally dissipated. He had never brought himself to believe that the child had really seen the Blessed Virgin, but he perpetually prayed that he might receive enlightenment regarding the truth. And his prayers were answered. The day came when he saw that the bent head of one of the young girls approaching the altar seemed encircled with an aureole. His startled glance followed her as she went back to the place in her pew; when she raised her head again he saw that it was Bernadette Soubirous.

All his perplexities ceased. The next day, in preaching to his parishioners, he said in a glad voice, "I have good news for you. Yesterday I began to understand that we could go confidently to the grotto." (24).

Bernadette herself was unaware of this great grace. Her life flowed on, tranquilly and for the most part aimlessly. She lived from day to day, feeling no immediate compulsion to do anything beyond the simple tasks entrusted to her and yearning for nothing beyond what she possessed. She had a gift with the sick. They responded almost miraculously to her care, and she had intuitive knowledge of their needs and their longings. She was happier at their bedsides, where everything was quiet, than she was in the crowded classrooms where her inadequate schooling made her a target for the jibes of the younger girls with whom she was inevitably placed. But when she could play with children, instead of competing with them in their lessons, she was a merry and congenial companion. She loved to jump rope. Later on she expressed regret that no such diversion was possible at the recreation hour.

She had been at the Hospice for several years when Monseigneur Forcade, the Bishop of Nevers, came to Lourdes. He was the Superior of the Motherhouse at Nevers of which the Hospice was a branch, and he had not been without ulterior motives in planning to visit the latter establishment. No sooner had he given his blessing to the community as a whole than he began to question the Superior about Bernadette. Some moments afterward, while he was being taken on a tour of inspection, he saw her in the kitchen. At the moment, she was cleaning carrots. Later he sent for her to come to the parlor and, almost without preamble, asked her if she had ever thought of a vocation for herself. She knew the general rule that no girl could enter an Order unless she possessed both an education and a dowry. She had neither, and she mentioned this quite simply. Then as the Bishop in his turn suggested that under special circumstances both these requirements could be waived, she added, "Besides, I am not good for anything." "You grate carrots very nicely," the Bishop told her.

The conversation closed on a note of encouragement
70

as far as the Bishop was concerned, but on one of hesitation from Bernadette. She said she would think the matter over. As a matter of fact, she had probably been thinking it over for some time already. As early as 1858, a local schoolteacher had written to her cousin, Abbé Rivière, who was a chaplain at Pau, "The Mayor and several other gentlemen have questioned Bernadette on the kind of calling she contemplates. After reflecting for a few minutes she replied that she would like to become a religious. 'You might change your mind,' rejoined the Mayor. 'In the meantime you must learn some sort of trade.' Then the little girl answered, 'I shan't change my mind. But I will do whatever my father and mother want me to.' "(25)

No one who came in contact with Bernadette could possibly consider her vacillating. Therefore she probably had no difficulty in convincing the Mayor that she knew her own mind, at least to the extent of feeling strongly that her destiny was in the cloister rather than beside the hearth. But it was not until long after this interview that she decided exactly where her obedience lay. According to her godmother, she secretly longed to become a Carmelite, but she had never permitted this hope to take form because she knew her health would not stand the rigors of that Order. Her asthma had become more and more troublesome and she was sometimes in bed for long periods. Her cousin, Jeanne Vedere, who afterward became a Trappiste herself, also declared that Bernadette desired to lead a cloistered and contemplative life, where the grille would automatically put an end to prying intruders and unwelcome visits and where she would be free to commune with her own soul and recapture her

71

radiant visions. It is easy to understand how much a secure withdrawal from annoyance would have meant to her, but she was too unselfish to run the risk of becoming a burden. She was also too considerate to disregard her benefactors. The members of many uncloistered congregations who came to Lourdes on pilgrimages sought her out and spoke to her cordially about coming to them. Unlettered, undowered and delicate as she was, she would have been a great acquisition for any one of them, and they knew it, though she, in her infinite humility, did not. The Sisters at the Hospice must have regarded these approaches with a certain amount of concern. Blessings always brighten as they take their flight, and the idea that Bernadette might be wrested from them gave her a new value in their eyes.

They need not have worried. She was very thankful for all they had done, and her good sense as well as her good taste told her that if she could not follow her heart's desire of retreating to a cloister, she should not desert one teaching and nursing congregation for another. In speaking to her cousin on the subject she said, "As I am not strong enough to enter the place I should have loved, I shall stay here. I am very fond of the Sisters of St. Vincent de Paul, but I should never have the courage to hurt the feelings of the Sisters of Nevers. Oh! I know it is not on account of my own poor little person that they want me to stay here. After all, what am I good for? What can anyone make out of me? But they have cared for me a long time and I must show my gratitude."

It was in the early part of 1866 that this conversation took place. On June 15 of the same year, she wrote to Nevers: "My dear Mother, I am happy to tell you that I

72

BERNADETTE IN THE SMALL ORATORY OF THE HOSPICE OF LOURDES

ENTRANCE TO THE CONVENT OF ST. GILDARD
THE MOTHERHOUSE AT NEVERS

have at last decided to enter our congregation. . . . I hope to leave here the beginning of next month."

The history of the congregation in question was a notable one. It had flourished ever since its foundation in 1680, at Saint-Saulge, a charming little city not far from Nevers, where its Motherhouse was later established. A pious Benedictine, Dom Jean-Baptiste de Laveyne, had established it with the collaboration of a young girl of the region named Marie Marchangy, who, like the good monk himself, left behind her a reputation for saintly living. Their first disciples wished to call themselves *"Sœurs de la Miséricorde"*—Sisters of Compassion. But the populace, with a familiarity that was half touching and half humorous, nicknamed them *"Sœurs de la Marmite"*—the soup-kettle Sisters! Their official title eventually became *"Sœurs de Charité et de l'Instruction Chrétienne de Nevers"*—Sisters of Charity and Christian Education of Nevers.

Marie Marchangy had ardently desired to provide and perpetuate for her followers an existence unifying the exercises of a contemplative life with those of an active one, and the manner in which she thought this might be done was duly set forth by the founder at the beginning of his pamphlet entitled *Avis Spirituel:* "Consider in the rules which are given you the two forms of life which you are to observe: One is that of Martha and the other is that of Mary. Martha is the personification of the active life, occupied by her duty to her neighbor as revealed through the need of charity, and Mary is the personification of a contemplative life, entirely devoted to the loving service of God. . . . To fill your active life you will have your care of the poor and sick, your instruction of children, your ordinary daily housework, your errands of mercy here and there, your conferences and various other sorts of practical action. To fill your contemplative life you will have your mental orisons, your prayers, your examinations of conscience, your frequent reception of the Sacraments, your studious reading, your discipline, and your consciousness of the nearness of God."

It is not surprising that this was the form of life upon which Bernadette finally decided, even if there had been no question of gratitude and familiarity involved. After all, she was essentially industrious, she loved little children and she understood all too well the needs of the poor. Probably prayer as a dominant occupation would have proved less satisfactory and less helpful, in her case, than prayer interspersed with work. At all events there is nothing to indicate that once having made her final choice, she ever regretted it.

She started on the fourth of July for Nevers, where all postulants of this congregation go to the Motherhouse for their training. Before this she had both the moment of triumph and the hour of anguish which Fate seems to reserve for every human being. Since she had gone to the Hospice to live, various scientists had been called in to pronounce upon the properties of the strange springs; and since these, upon analysis, had been found neither beneficent nor harmful, the conclusion had been reached that they must be miraculous, since cures continued to take place. A commission had also been named to make a complete review of the general situation; at the instigation of the Bishop of Tarbes, doctors, chemists and geologists had been invited to join with scholarly clerics in order that no clue should be neglected which might

74

throw light on the subject and help in arriving at the truth, whatever this might be. Once organized, the commission itself asked for "the collaboration of time," and deliberated for three months, though four years had already been devoted to intensive research. Bernadette was summoned to appear before it, and the candor and simplicity of her manner, as well as the clarity and precision with which she expressed herself, made a profound impression. The different members of the commission went to the grotto with her and encouraged her to describe the wonders she had witnessed with the realism which such visits facilitated. Her representation of the sixteenth apparition was so especially moving that one prelate at least furtively wiped away tears as he listened to her. This account probably formed the last link in the chain of favorable evidence. For the verdict of the commission, rendered on January 18, 1862, read as follows:

"We hold that the Immaculate Mary, Mother of God, actually appeared to Bernadette Soubirous on the eleventh of February, 1858, and on the days following, to the number of eighteen times, in the grotto of Massabielle, near the town of Lourdes; that this apparition bears all the signs of authenticity and that the faithful are free to consider it true."

Having granted the reality of the apparitions, the next step was logical: the chapel mystically demanded must indubitably be built. In a mandate issued by Monseigneur Laurence he stated: "In order to conform to the wish of the Blessed Virgin, several times expressed at the time of the apparitions, we propose to build a sanctuary on the ground adjoining the grotto which has now become the property of the Diocese of Tarbes."

In May, 1866, the crypt for the Basilica of Notre Dame de Lourdes was dedicated, and Bernadette took part in the triumphal procession which formed part of the ceremony, wearing the white dress and blue sash of the Children of Mary. When the statue of the Virgin, carved by the famous sculptor Fabisch, had been enshrined in the grotto, three years earlier, she had been ailing and she had not been present, though conceivably she might have gone if some real effort had been made to get her there comfortably. By a strange chance, the Abbé Peyramale had been ill also; therefore, he himself did not see the first of the predicted processions, at the possibility of which he had so scoffed, and he had been less philosophical over his enforced absence than Bernadette herself. She was remarkably resigned to her disappointment, but with characteristic drollery she had remarked, "Monsieur Peyramale forbade me to take part in the procession. The Virgin noticed this, and she sent him a good sharp pain which prevented him from going himself."

At the time of the second great processional, however, neither illness nor resentment robbed Bernadette of her vindication and her victory. She tasted of both to the full. The celebration was far more than clerical: it was communal. Triumphal arches curved over the main avenues of Lourdes and the houses were almost covered with garlands. The town was abloom with flowers. The ceremonial cortege formed in the parish church and advanced toward the grotto to the sound of choral singing. The Bishop appeared on the heights, preceded by an escort of canons. An enormous crowd, following after, surged all around him. On the high altar placed in front of the statue in the grotto the pontifical Mass began. At the

Elevation the silence of the crowd was profound. Only the flowing of the Gave made a sound. It was the great hour of a great day. The Son of Mary descended to the place where His Mother had been. The glory of His presence penetrated to the obscure place which Bernadette had chosen for her own.

So much for the moment of triumph; the hour of anguish was still to come. On the beautiful summer evening preceding her departure for Nevers she went back to the grotto for the last time, and her customary composure deserted her completely. She clung to the base of the niche, kissing it passionately, uncontrolled tears streaming down her face, her slim little shoulders shaken with sobs. The Sister who was with her, having left her in peace as long as she dared, at length became alarmed. Going up to her quietly, she laid her hand on the young girl's arm. Then, as Bernadette continued to weep convulsively, the Sister spoke to her in a gentle voice.

"Bernadette, why do you grieve so? Don't you know that the Virgin is everywhere, and that she will always be your mother?"

"Oh, I know it, I know it! But here at Lourdes, this grotto has been my heaven!"

Her heaven. She could visualize no other, she yearned for no other. And she was leaving heaven behind her; she was going into exile. It was the end of everything. Or so it seemed to her.

But it was not the end of everything. The idyl indeed was over. She had ceased to be a shepherdess. But she had become a Sister.

PART TWO

The Sister

❀ EIGHT ❀

Wᴇɴ Bernadette left Lourdes, she had never seen a city. She had been only on brief infrequent excursions to Pau and Baguerès and Cauterets. Her dear and familiar haunts were a silent pasture, a mystic grotto and a sequestered garden. But Bordeaux, her first stopping place on the way to Nevers, did not bewilder her. It delighted her. A friend, Leontine Muret, and the Superior of the Hospice were her companions on the journey. They left Lourdes in the morning and arrived in Bordeaux "that same evening," which was rapid traveling for the time. They remained there for two days before they went on to Périgueux, and Bernadette wrote home about her experience zestfully:

"They took us to visit all the houses of the congregation, chief among them the Institution Impériale. It is more like a palace than a religious house; it is not at all like the Hospice at Lourdes. We went to see the Carmelite Church and from there to the waterfront of the Garonne to see the boats, and afterward to the Botanical Garden. We have beheld a great novelty, just guess what? Red, black, white and gray fishes! What I admired the most was seeing these little creatures swimming around without any fear in the presence of a crowd of street urchins who were watching them."

Superficially considered, this seems like an ingenuous comment. Actually, it is ingenuous only in form; its significance is profound. It gives tongue to the deep distaste which Bernadette herself possessed for any sort of publicity, especially publicity tinged with ridicule or malice, her inability to overcome this, and her wonder that any sort of being could do so. Her admiration for the fish, though different in kind from her admiration for the Institution Impériale, was almost as great. Probably she was overawed by the latter, which is indeed most nobly housed, and which to this day—it is now called the Institution Nationale des Sourdes-Muettes—is one of the finest schools of its kind for the training of deaf-mutes. But she really enjoyed the fish.

Apparently nothing of note happened at Périgueux. At least nothing seems to have been recorded. The little group left there at ten in the morning on Saturday, July 9, and arrived at Nevers at half-past ten that same evening. It must have been a terribly tedious journey; and though the tired travelers were duly met at the station by one of the high quaint carriages belonging to the congregation, their reception at the Motherhouse itself was anything but cheering. It was not the custom of the Superior General to receive new arrivals when they came in at night; and the Mistress of the Novices at the moment was barely convalescent after a long illness and was not able to sit up. Bernadette was conducted to the largest dormitory of all, the *dortoir* St. Marie. She was obliged to traverse its entire length in order to reach the bed which had been assigned
82

her. The sound of her own footsteps, echoing from the bare floor to the high ceiling, must have frightened her; the way which led through the vastness must have seemed interminable to her tired feet; the mysterious movements of the white curtains concealing the beds along the way must have betrayed the curiosity of the peeping girls behind them. But her own bed was close beside a statue of the Virgin. When she saw this, she forgot her weariness and her fear. She cuddled down, content.

It was two days before the Mother General sent for Bernadette, and when she did a conversation ensued which ran something like this:

"Are you the postulant from Lourdes?"

"Yes, Reverend Mother."

"What is your name?"

"Bernadette Soubirous."

"What can you do?"

"Nothing very much, Reverend Mother."

"But, my child, what are we to do with you then?"

Bernadette did not reply.

"Who is it who has recommended you to us?"

"The Bishop of Nevers."

"Ah, that holy man has sent us many others. Come, my child, I will take you to the refectory where you will have supper with the Lourdes' Sisters; then tomorrow morning, if you are not too tired, you will go to the kitchen and help the lay Sister to wash up."(26)

Of course the Mother General was much better informed and much more moved than she admitted. But she had decided that Bernadette must be treated like any other postulant, with a slight extra stress on the value of humility; and the Sisters with whom she had conferred

83

had, on the whole, agreed with her that this was a wise plan. Indeed, there had been a division of opinion as to the wisdom of admitting Bernadette to the Motherhouse at all. The younger and more progressive element was the most enthusiastic about it, while the postulants and novices were all atwitter with the thought of having a celebrity in their midst, and they were not entirely alone in this. There were others who felt her presence would give great prestige to the convent, that it would attract much favorable attention, and that many young girls, wavering on the brink of a vocation, would find their feelings crystallized at the thought of being in such unique company. The Sisters who subscribed to this school of thought were less exuberant than the younger group, but their gravity was tinged with pride and pleasure. The elder and more conservative element in the congregation, however, had its doubts. Melanie Mathieu, one of the "children of the Salette," had gone to five different convents in succession and had not fitted into any one of them; this seemed to indicate that young and ardent mystics might prove unadaptable to community life. Moreover, there was the question of Bernadette's health. She coughed a great deal. She was possibly consumptive as well as asthmatic; she might become a charge herself, instead of serving to nurse others. Finally, there was this question of humility which was so all important. It seemed unlikely that the recipient of such rare grace as she had received could be unaffected by it. It might be difficult to subdue her spirit and curb her pride.

The Sisters need not have worried. Bernadette, as everyone now knows, was essentially tractable, essentially uncomplaining and essentially lowly. What she needed was praise, not discouragement. She was convinced already of her own insignificance, and she required release from the burden of this conviction. If she could have been given a sense of dignity, instead of a sense of disgrace, she would have responded to it touchingly, she would have expanded as naturally and beautifully as a flower, and her very surroundings would have shone with her reflected sweetness. As it was, she shrank farther and farther into herself.

The Mistress of the Novices, Mère Marie Thérèse Vauzou, had been among those prepared to welcome Bernadette warmly, but she had expected warmth in return. She visualized herself as the newcomer's confidante no less than her mentor; she foresaw privileged and intimate hours with her. It had been agreed that Bernadette should tell the story of the apparitions to the congregation as a whole, but that after she had done this the subject was not to be brought up again. This plan was pleasing to Bernadette. She presented herself, still dressed like a little Pyrenean peasant, and accepted, with her usual complete composure, the place appointed to her before the assembly; then she related her experiences with the same sincerity and simplicity which she had always shown in speaking of them. She did not expect or intend to speak of them again. But Mère Marie Thérèse did not have the same expectations and intentions. She had thought that in her case an exception would be made to the rule that had been laid down. When she found that Bernadette was not receptive to such a program, Mère Marie Thérèse may have been astonished and a little piqued. She meant to be just. This is clear from her own memorandum of the novice as "modest, pious and devout, with a real sense of order." But to this apt characterization, she added the word "stiff." Thwarted in her original plan, which she had kept more or less to herself, she subscribed, at least outwardly, to the general idea that humiliation was wholesome for Bernadette.

The young girl's submission to disparagement was so satisfactory that her probation period was almost unbelievably brief. She remained only twenty days among the "Little Bonnets," as the postulants at the Motherhouse in Nevers are colloquially called, because of their quaint headdress, frilled around the face and tied under the chin, like a baby's cap. They were not happy days. She was terribly homesick in her strange surroundings; she longed unutterably for the Gave and the grotto. The mere sight of a letter from home brought tears to her eyes, and when she had succeeded in seeking out a secret place, she wept unrestrainedly as she read the missive. This nostalgia wounded her in a way that held no healing for her, but it was destined to bring calm to many desolate girls in years to come. For Bernadette never forgot her own loneliness and her own longing; therefore she never forgot, either, to assuage the loneliness and the longing which was the lot of others. "You will get accustomed to all this very soon," she used to whisper, with a comforting caress, when she saw that a "Little Bonnet" was bowed or heard sounds suspiciously like sobbing coming from it. "Everyone is very good and kind here. If you are homesick come to see me in the infirmary."

Those who took her at her word were charmed as well as cheered by the reception which she gave them when they invaded her solitude and interrupted her needlework. Their feeling for her, in many cases, approached

86

adoration. They kissed her veil surreptitiously and gazed soulfully into her eyes. She discouraged such rapturous acts with quiet admonitions, severe only in their implication. "Mademoiselle, you know that is not allowed. . . ." "My child, do not look at me like that." All effusiveness was distasteful to her, but she suppressed her instinct to recoil visibly from it. She was kindness itself to all the novices, and much as she loved to be alone, she never regarded the arrival of the "Little Bonnets" as an intrusion. Several of the girls so befriended have told stories of her loving-kindness to them in their own words. "Once I was in the cloister on the St. Gertrude's side of the convent," relates a former postulant who later became Mother Marguerite, "when I had been at the Motherhouse only four or five days and was terribly homesick. A little Sister came along, her veil falling far forward, hiding her shoulders. She walked straight into the midst of the 'Little Bonnets' and asked, 'Which is the latest postulant? . . . , 'I am, dear Sister,' I answered. I was instantly very much struck with her sweet smile and something extraordinary about her personality which I could not define. Then she said, 'And are you homesick?' just as if she had taken it for granted, or as if God Himself had shed special light on my case. I answered with complete candor, 'Oh, yes, very!' She put her hand on my shoulder. 'Come, come, you must not worry,' she said. 'I know that you will persevere in the congregation.' "(27)

She knew it because her own gifts had been "crowned with grace to persevere." After her brief postulancy, she took the habit on July 29, 1866. Three months later, the Bishop was suddenly aroused in the night with the news that she was dying and that she desired to make her profession on her deathbed. He rose and rushed to the Motherhouse, where he found her in a state of anguish. She had been seized by severe spasms; she was almost suffocating; there had been hemorrhages as well as constriction—in short, all the worst aspects of a critical case of asthma. Of course she could not talk. But when Monseigneur Forcade had himself recited the formula of vows, she bent her head and managed to murmur amen. The Bishop spoke a few appropriate words, blessed her and departed, fully expecting that he would never see her alive again. But Bernadette had extraordinary rallying powers, as she proved repeatedly; her vitality, which seemed so low, was actually strong and resilient. Before long, she had managed to raise herself in bed, which always made breathing much easier for her. Once she had succeeded in doing this, she also succeeded in speaking. She triumphantly announced that she was sure she was not going to die that night after all.

The manner in which the Mother General answered certainly sounds very harsh, read after all these years. Authorities do not differ over her actual words. She seems to have said, "What! You knew you were not going to die tonight and you did not tell me so! What a little fool you are! If you are not dead by morning, I shall take away your new veil and dress you like a novice again!" It may be, of course, that even at a moment as poignant as this, Mère Josephine Imbert felt she could not mitigate the severity of the program of Bernadette's humiliation to which she was pledged. But it seems much more likely that in her relief and astonishment she spoke half jestingly, and that it is only because her words, and not her tone, have been preserved, that they seem so cold and

SISTER MARIE BERNARD (BERNADETTE SOUBIROUS)

THE INFIRMARY OF THE HOLY CROSS

cruel. Be that as it may, Bernadette's own answer was priceless. "Just as you like, of course, Reverend Mother," she said with a smile. Her sense of humor must always have been her saving grace.

Bernadette kept her veil spread out on her bed and received the congratulations of her companions on its acquisition. But later she resumed her novitiate and it continued her normal course. She made her public profession with the rest of her class a year later. Her conduct had been exemplary throughout. Her bearing during the great ceremony was unforgettable. She was the last to pronounce her vows. As she knelt before the Host, her voice, usually so hushed and timid, rang through the chapel with triumphant clarity as she spoke the irrevocable words:

"I, Sister Marie Bernard Soubirous, pledge myself and promise to my God that as long as I have happiness to be in the Congregation of Sisters of Charity and Christian Instruction established at Nevers under the authority of His Excellence the Bishop, I will fulfill the promises of the vows of poverty, chastity, obedience and charity, in the way whereby they are defined in the Rule of the Sisters. I pray our Saviour Jesus Christ through the intercession of the Blessed Virgin, our Holy Mother, to give me grace to perfect them and to fulfill them. Amen."

One of the Sisters said years later, "I have the most vivid memory of Sister Marie Bernard's voice as she took her vows. It was firm, but very sweet and entirely devoid of self-consciousness. In the tribune, the members of the choir were so moved that they held their breath in order to hear her better."

There is nothing to indicate that Bernadette, who at

the conclusion of this service had become Sister Marie Bernard, held her own breath. Indeed, she seems to have been as collected as usual, even during the trying scene which ensued. After the religious ceremony in the chapel, there was another, scarcely less solemn, in the Great Hall of the Novitiate. Here the Bishop presented to each of the newly professed Sisters a crucifix, a book containing the constitution of the congregation, and "a letter of obedience," in which the appointment for future service which she had received was duly outlined. Bernadette alone received no such letter.

There was always a great deal of interest and curiosity beforehand concerning the appointments which would be made. Some of the young Sisters remained at Nevers. Some were sent to the superb Institution Impériale at Bordeaux which had so greatly impressed Bernadette. Others were assigned to the Hospice at Lourdes. Still others were sent to small country schools to teach. The Motherhouse reached out all over France to salvage, to nurse and to instruct. Each of the girls was naturally eager to know what her lot would be, a plum or a privation. But it did not occur to any that she would be purposely slighted or overlooked altogether; she regarded definite and honorable occupation as certain. However, when all her classmates had been summoned by name before the Bishop, Bernadette was still left standing patiently and expectantly in her corner, her pleasant little face more and more puzzled. Monseigneur Forcade duly made inquiry.

"Why has Sister Marie Bernard not been presented? Why have I been given no letter of obedience for her?"

It appears that he knew perfectly well, that he and

Mère Josephine had rehearsed their little comedy beforehand. She took up the cue.

"Monseigneur, it was not possible to give her an assignment. She is a stupid little creature. She does not do anything well."

The Bishop made a sign to Bernadette. She came and knelt down before him.

"So you cannot do anything well, Sister Marie Bernard?"

"The Reverend Mother says so and she cannot be mistaken. Therefore it must be true."

"But, my poor child, what are we going to do with you then? What will be the use of having you in the congregation?"

"That is what I asked you myself in Lourdes, Monseigneur. I told you I was not good for anything. And you said I could grate carrots very nicely."

❀ NINE ❀

Bᴇʀɴᴀᴅᴇᴛᴛᴇ had sealed her own fate. She was sent back to the kitchen to grate more carrots.

This did not happen immediately. The Bishop had been rendered speechless by the quickness of her retort. But the Mother General, recovering swiftly from her own surprise, came to his assistance.

"If you approve, Monseigneur, we could keep her here at the Motherhouse out of charity and find some sort of work for her at the infirmary. As she is almost always ailing herself, this ought to be congenial work for her. To begin with, she would simply be put in charge of cleaning. Afterward, she could prepare beverages, if we can find a way to teach her how to make them."

Marie Bernard was quite capable of preparing beverages, as the Mother General was well aware. The young Sister had the same aptitude for household tasks as she had for needlework, and her natural gift for nursing had increased with time. Her patience stood her in good stead and also the experience she had acquired in helping to care for her brood of younger brothers. Her own respect for obedience was communicable. Refractory patients quickly became tractable when she cared for them; so did two or three elderly Sisters who were "mentally afflicted" and whom no one else could manage. She had "healing hands," not in any miraculous sense, but in the sense that they were sure and soothing—the hands of a "born nurse." She kept the atmosphere of the infirmary cheerful by her sunny serenity and she felt neither fear nor repugnance in the presence of death. The dying drew on her fortitude and faith and she could make a shroud seem like a garment of glory. The doctor under whom she worked was loud in his praises of her.

"She has a calm and gentle nature, suited to the care of the sick," he declared. "Besides, she shows real intelligence in her nursing, and is careful to see that prescriptions are scrupulously carried out. Her discipline is excellent. For my part, I have complete confidence in her."

He had no occasion to change his opinion during the eight years that Bernadette's work kept her in the infirmary. At the end of this time it was decided to transfer her to the sacristy because of her own slowly but surely failing health. Almost the only expression of envy to which she had ever given tongue had been voiced when the "obedience" of a companion took this Sister to a hospital, and she was sorry to leave her own sick. Neither can there be any doubt that they were sorrier still to see her go and that she suffered additionally because of their grief. But the care of fine linens, rich vestments and sacred vessels was also well suited to her spirit. She had a natural "taste for the divine" and these were the outward and visible signs of divine ministry and divine grace. The preparation of the Christmas *crèche* was a task which she always undertook with skill and sympathy, and the

93

figurines which she disposed so delicately to form the scene of the Nativity were very real to her. One night, as she was placing the image of the tiny Christ child in the miniature manger, she murmured tenderly, "I am afraid you are very cold, little Jesus, in this Bethlehem stable! The people who would not give you shelter must have been very heartless!" Undoubtedly the thought had flashed through her mind that the shepherds "abiding in the fields, keeping watch over their flocks by night" would have been more kind to the Lamb of God. She was far from the hillside at Bartrès, and there were those who said of her that "she did not like to talk about the past." But she had not forgotten it.

After the midnight Mass of Christmas Eve, when the congregation, according to its custom, departed to rest, one of its number remained motionless in her seat. She seemed so lost to all sense of her surroundings, so enfolded by the divine, that the Sister who had charge of closing the chapel did not have the heart to wrest her from her prayers. She left the worshiper in peace, but she herself waited and watched. Long afterward, the remote figure rose from her knees and with a look of wonder, as if she had wakened from a happy dream, slipped away to her cell, gliding through the shadows in such a way that her black habit made her almost invisible. But the waiting Sister saw that it was Bernadette.

The sacristy had one grave disadvantage from Marie Bernard's point of view: it was easily accessible to strangers. Although they did not know that she herself was the sacristan, they penetrated to her preserves, clamoring to see her. "Won't you please go and tell Sister Marie Bernard that I want very much to meet her?" one imperious lady demanded. "Certainly, madame. I will let her know at once," Bernadette replied, and promptly disappeared as if in search of an unknown Sister. Pleas were no more moving to her than orders. "It would mean everything to me if I could catch just a glimpse of Sister Marie Bernard," begged another visitor, less exacting, but equally intrusive. "Very well, madame. Be so good as to watch the garden gate. I happen to know that she will pass through it in just a minute." Bernadette slipped away, leaving the caller in an attitude of alert attention. Half an hour later, another Sister, coming in, found her still wide eyed and tense.

"Can I do anything for you, madame?" she asked courteously. "Oh, no, thank you. I am waiting to see Sister Marie Bernard pass through the garden gate. The quiet little Sister who was here when I came—I don't know her name—very kindly told me I need wait only a minute, that she would be going through there very soon." The newcomer smiled. "And didn't the quiet little Sister with whom you talked go through the gate herself almost instantly?" she inquired. For a moment the caller stared at her speechlessly. Then she understood.

There was no question of Marie Bernard's competence in dealing with cases like these. But she did not enjoy them. She had been wholly sincere in saying, "I have come here to hide myself," when she first arrived at the Motherhouse. "My place is like that of a broom after it has been used—behind the door!" she often stated gaily. She had gone so far as to ask to be excused from going to the parlor, which was much more formidable than the one at the Hospice in Lourdes, and except on rare occasions her wishes in this matter were respected. In church, with one swift graceful motion, she arranged her veil in such a way as to conceal her face. "It gives me a private chapel all my own," she said by way of explanation. But she could not hide in the sacristy. She was relieved when she was taken away from it. After that her appointed tasks were humbler. She was the happier on that account. They left her spirit free to soar.

She sang now, as she went about her work—not hymns and psalms, but the poignant folk song of her native Pyrenees in her own *patois*. Her duties were by no means confined to the kitchen. She resumed her fine needlework, for which she had never lost her dexterity and her predilection. One of her few recorded remarks which reveals impatience was made to a careless laundress who had torn her linen undergarments. "Now I shall have to mend them!" she said reprovingly. But there is no doubt that she enjoyed doing this, and her apology was as spontaneous as her rebuke had been.

Once a mother, whose little boy was very ill, brought a cradle cover she had just begun to the Motherhouse and, with tears in her eyes, asked that Sister Marie Bernard might be allowed to work on it. She was convinced that if this could be done, the baby would get well. The portress, Sister Victoria, having consulted the Mother General, took the coverlet to a group of Sisters who were sitting together—Marie Bernard among them—and inquired if any of them would be willing to straighten out the pattern for Madame X, who had become tangled up in it and had sent out an appeal for help. Then, apparently by accident, she extended the coverlet in Marie Bernard's general direction. "How convenient it is for these fine ladies to hand over the fancywork they spoil for someone else to fix up!" Bernadette exclaimed, her pride as an expert needlewoman instantly aroused. "Come, give it to me, I will be glad to do what I can with it." The coverlet did not leave her hands again until after it was finished in beautiful form. Meanwhile the sick child recovered.

An allied art, for which she showed great aptitude, and which she was encouraged to cultivate, was that of folding veils into effective pleats. It came to be the custom among the novices to vie with each other in securing her services, especially when they were dressing for the ceremony of taking the habit, and the dormitories of St. Marie and St. Anne, usually so still and spotless, were all aflutter with excitement. Bernadette always entered into the spirit of the day. "The cornets I put on hold firm," she used to say, as she fastened the white headdresses above the eager young faces; and the double meaning in her words was not lost on the girls whom she coifed. Her interest did not end when she had seen a novice first transformed into a nun; she watched her searchingly for several days afterward, to find out how far her unaccustomed fingers would prove naturally expert; and when Marie Bernard was not satisfied with what she saw, she took immediate steps to correct it. "Oh, Sister! How badly you are coifed!" she exclaimed one day, when she came face to face with Thérèse Portal, then a new-made nun, in one of the cloisters. "Come in here with me."

"Here" was St. Adelaide's hall, the nearest vacant apartment. Bernadette drew Thérèse inside and took her headdress completely apart. Then she replaced the long cornet, fastened the regulation pin under the chin, and laid the veil over its white linen foundation at the exact distance from the forehead stipulated by the rules of the Order. Having put a second pin in the crown to secure this veil, her final act was to pleat its folds so that they would flow gracefully over her subject's shoulders. Then, standing back a little to look the girl over, she said with approval, "Now you are a real Sister of Nevers!"

Even on her deathbed she did not lose interest in such arrangements. According to custom, she wore her own veil when she received Communion; but it was usually a novice who prepared her for this Sacrament, and Bernadette, without being exigent, was particular concerning this preparation. She still saw to it that the folds were properly pleated, so that they should fall gracefully over the shoulders; and to accomplish this end, she spread the veil out over the bed and gave the novice an object lesson. "Since you will so soon be wearing a veil of your own," she said, with a tact which robbed her gesture of all captiousness, "it is fitting that I should show you just how to do so."

Her taste and her skill in these matters were unquestionable; and the recognition she received for them—a distinct departure from the prevailing policy of disparagement—led to varied accomplishments. On the "Day of Doves," which came directly after the feast of the Sacred Heart, Sister Marie Bernard undertook a special sort of handiwork. A great processional always occurred at this time and the chapel and cloister were devoutly decorated for it. Once a young nun who was wreathing the sacred spots with the absorption which characterized this labor of love was startled by a sudden summons from the mistress of novices.

"Sister, Marie Bernard needs someone to help her.

Suppose you go to her. You will find her in the dormitory of the Holy Angels."

The girl could hardly wait to finish draping the garland she held before rushing off to seize her unexpected opportunity. Later on, she described the experience which awaited her in her own words: "I was thrilled at the thought of helping Bernadette, of working with her. I ran to the dormitory of the Holy Angels and found our dear Sister seated before a table covered with cardboard, wadding, gauze and white feathers—the last the plenteous plumage of our pigeons, which at the time completely filled the dovecots at the Motherhouse. Sister explained the work to me. The requirement was to achieve dovelike ornaments which would serve as symbols of faithful souls. The cardboard was already cut in the general shape of birds, but it still needed to be trimmed with cotton and covered with gauze, preparatory to beginning the most delicate part of the task: piercing this spongy substance with the feathers and thus transfiguring it into mystic doves suited to adorn the statues and the altars.

"As a matter of fact, my share in this artistic work was most modest. I was supposed only to arrange the feathers according to size and place them before Sister. It was she who took them one by one and placed them with skill, the largest to form the wings and the tail, the smallest for the breast and back of each dove. She did this rapidly and adroitly, observing the rule of silence as she worked. As far as I was concerned, I can assure you that I was far less intrigued with the doves than with our dear Sister. Discretion and respect prevented me from looking her straight in the face. But I followed the movements of her flexible hands as I thought how proud I should be to tell my companions, during recreation, that I had worked the whole evening with Bernadette.

"The first dove which emerged from our joint efforts was not a masterpiece. Sister Marie Bernard looked it over, made a little grimace, and said smilingly, 'That is not a dove, it is a toad!' The toad was cast aside, but our apprenticeship had been served on it. The other doves we made, half a dozen in all, were a credit to our craft, especially the smallest one. Bernadette noticed that I admired this and told me so. 'I do too,' she said, adding in a whisper, 'It is the littlest.' It was only later I learned that she had a special tenderness for the very small. But even at the moment I was enthralled as she added, 'We will give it the best place of all—on the arm of Christ the Saviour, near the Sacred Heart.' Then she spoke to the bird itself. 'What a happy fate is yours, little bird! How I wish I were in your place!'

"Gently, as if the mystic dove, palpitating with life, had fluttered between her fingers, she kissed its two wings. I understood that her gesture had not been a caress for a bird but a salute to a symbol. And I thanked God in the secret places of my own heart for the simplicity and the candor which He bestowed on children and on saints."(28)

To me this little story of the "Day of Doves" is perhaps the most exquisite among all I have found which center on Marie Bernard's handiwork. But this took many forms. She made a model of the grotto at Lourdes as delicate and exquisite as the Christmas crèche. She learned to paint little pictures, depicting both the happy Christ child and the Man of Sorrows crowned with thorns, touchingly and convincingly. She also decorated Easter eggs for

100

friends and patrons of the congregation with drawings done in relief against a background of color. She was faintly amused at the amount of praise with which she was showered for etching anything so simple; indeed, she seems to have put it in the same class with the carrots, for she spoke of it in much the same way. "Oh! don't talk to me about it! I might just as well earn my way to heaven by grating eggshells as by doing anything else!" she said gaily.

She jested with her companions now, easily and light-heartedly, as she had bantered her schoolmates at the Hospice. While it was true, as one of the Sisters said, "that she never spoke two words if one would do," that one word was always *le mot juste*.(29) She thoroughly enjoyed the hour of recreation. This began with a canticle, sung in unison by the Sisters as they clustered around a statue of the Virgin; then, as they dispersed, they walked in smaller groups around the garden which the statue adorned. One of Bernadette's contemporaries told of saying to her as they stood together near the shrine, "You are like me, aren't you? You love this statue. It inspires you when you pray before it"—and of Bernadette's significant reply, "I wasn't looking at the statue while I prayed. I was looking higher up."

Another contemporary gave us a vivid description of an outstanding promenade: "One day at recreation time I was walking with Sister Marie Bernard and a novice whom I must describe to you. Her name was Sister Angelique Gemmel, and Monseigneur Forcade had brought her to us from Guadaloupe. She was a Creole, who spoke French with the strange accent of the Antilles, and who had been nicknamed 'The English Girl' for this reason.

Bernadette liked to walk with her, perhaps because she found her temperamentally congenial, but certainly also because of the pleasure which this exotic French language gave her. Sometimes she laughed until she cried over it, and Sister Angelique laughed, too, at her own mistakes.

"We left the novices' parterre which we called Notre Dame de Force and went down into the garden by the path of Notre Dame des Eaux. All at once a bat, which had been circling over our heads, alighted on a vegetable patch a few feet from us. Our 'English Girl' was not familiar with this kind of creature. She thought it was a bird and leaped forward to catch it. I cried out to her, 'Don't touch the horrid thing! A bat! There is nothing in the world more hideous! It is an image of the Devil!' Sister Angelique, who had already caught hold of her 'bird,' immediately let go of it and backed away, covered with confusion.

"It was then that Bernadette turned to me and gave me a lesson in theology. It was not her habit to go in for dissertations or to act learned—she was far too simple for that! But it did sometimes happen that in the form of a retort or on the occasion of some incident, she would say something that was so full of good sense that it made me reflect for a long time afterward. This was never premeditated on her part; the occasion produced the proverb. All her sayings which are quoted nowadays were brought forth in this way, thanks to that lively wit of hers, which made everything she said so kindly.

"What she said then, with a deliberate gravity which was very striking, was this: 'A bat, the image of the Devil! One of God's own creatures, the image of the Devil! No indeed! Everything that God has done is well done and

102

does not resemble the Devil. There is only one thing which resembles the Devil, and that is sin.' "

Bernadette's rare excursions into the outside world were occasions of even more lighthearted enjoyment than the pleasant but restricted hours of recreation at the Motherhouse. Once when she had gone with several other young Sisters to spend the day at Coulanges, at a country house belonging to the school of Our Lady of the Angels, she seemed unusually happy. She loved the solitude of the place and its peace. She showed an "almost childlike joy" in walking through its avenues of trees and in sitting beside the bank of the river which flowed near it. Her black habit and stiff headdress and the small starched tabs sticking out over her breast did not bother her any more; she wore them as easily as her striped kerchief and her Pyrenean cloak. She sang her little Bigourdane songs and did a bit of fine needlework as she sat there. She said it all reminded her of Lourdes. In the middle of the afternoon a messenger arrived from the Motherhouse to say that some Bishops had come to visit. The truants were recalled; indeed, they were awaited. The message was tactfully worded to include all the young Sisters, though of course it was only Bernadette whom the eminent ecclesiastics really wanted to see. She knew that she would not be able to escape the dreaded parlor.

"Those good Bishops would have done much better to stay in their own dioceses and let us stay here!" she said rebelliously, as she gathered up her belongings and rose from the riverbank.

The Franco-Prussian War affected her poignantly, as indeed it affected the entire congregation. Its members

103

did not remain withdrawn from the conflict, as a cloistered Order could do, to some extent. In 1870 the Sisters of Nevers at the four Houses in Paris obtained permission from the Superior General to remain at their posts throughout the siege. They considered this the greatest favor which could be shown them, since it gave them a chance of dying in the performance of their duties and thus testifying to the faith that was in them. They were entirely self-forgetful, devoting themselves, day and night, to bandaging the wounded, nursing the sick and consoling the dying. Several of them succumbed to typhus and smallpox, which they caught from their patients. Their heroic example, even more than their pious precepts, resulted in numerous conversions and many "Christian deaths" were attributed to them.

From afar, Marie Bernard followed the consecrated task of her successful Sisters. She withdrew more and more into the silences which solaced her. There was nothing she herself could do except to pray, but she did that. One of her biographers(30) has likened the form and effect of her prayers to the manners and methods of a peasant who, in his youth, served as shepherd at the manor of Villaine, where wild boars constantly threatened the harvest with their ravages. The boy had no weapons. But every evening he took his rustic flute and seated himself on the borderline between the dark forest, whence the danger came, and the ripening wheat fields, which glistened like gold under the mellow moon. All night long he sat there and played the simple tunes which were the only ones he knew. But they sufficed. Their melody pierced the silences of the wood and kept the boars at bay.

To me this comparison is apt as well as exquisite. The

THE CHAPEL OF SAINT BERNADETTE

THE CANONIZATION OF SAINT BERNADETTE IN
ST. PETER'S, IN ROME

young shepherd felt no animosity toward the boars; he did not wish to harm them, only to save the harvest. In like measure, Bernadette did not feel too harshly toward the Prussians. "I know they are doing their duty," she said sadly, realizing that the soldiers had no choice but to go where they were sent. She seems also to have felt that, to a certain extent, France was expiating its own sins, and that it must work out its own salvation. The Third Empire was a period of great luxury and frivolity; the cloister and the court were inevitably far apart, and in many religious circles there was a strong conviction that just chastisement was being meted out.

One day in late October, the pale autumnal sky was suddenly flooded with dark lurid red, the color of blood. Its effect and its symbolism were unmistakable. The entire community at Nevers assembled on the terrace to watch it and to wait anxiously for its passing. Some of the Sisters were terribly frightened. Bernadette was not among these. But as she gazed at the strange somber clouds, she accepted them unquestioningly as an omen and a warning.

"And to think," she exclaimed sadly and compassionately, "that there are still people who resist conversion!"

Tumult of a sort had taken possession of her quiet soul. But still she was not frightened, even when the Prussians came closer and closer to Nevers. The Chevalier Gougenot des Mousseaux, who came to break the bad news, received a negative answer when he asked her if she were not alarmed. She spoke with such obvious tranquillity and sincerity that he went on questioning her, his curiosity and his admiration both aroused.

"So you think there is nothing to fear?"

"I am afraid only of bad Catholics."

"Really? Not anything else at all?"

"No, Monsieur."

She meant it. Perhaps her courage, which proved contagious, played its own small part in saving Nevers, for danger has a way of retreating before those who confront it calmly and casually, whereas it pounces mercilessly on those who cower before it. Be that as it may, the Prussian advance was checked. The alien army, which had been sweeping over the countryside, leaving death and disaster in its wake, never succeeded in entering Nevers. But Bernadette did not gloat over its escape. She continued to center her concern on soldiers' souls rather than on their successes.

"Oh!" she wrote to the Superior of the Hospice at Lourdes. "We should weep rather than rejoice to see our unfortunate country so blind and so obdurate. Let us pray constantly for these poor sinners that they may be converted. Let us ask Our Saviour and the Blessed Virgin to change these savage wolves into gentle sheep."

In mind and spirit she was still very close to the hillside at Bartrès after all. Another young girl—Joan of Domremy—had tended flocks before she had saved France. Bernadette did not know that she belonged in Joan's glorious company and in the glorious company of Heaven, where, no doubt, Joan was among the first to welcome her. But she did know that the Saviour of all the world was also the Good Shepherd, that He would protect His flock, and that He would draw into the fold again all those who had strayed far from it but who returned penitently, seeking salvation.

106

❂ TEN ❂

"What shall I tell you about myself? I am in my little white chapel all the time now. Nevertheless, these last three weeks I have been able to go to Mass on Sunday, though I have gone back to bed immediately afterward. I have completely lost the use of my limbs and have to submit to being carried in an armchair. But the Sisters do this so cheerfully that it really does not seem like much of a humiliation. I am always afraid that they will hurt themselves. But they laugh and say that they could carry four like me."

As we have already learned, Bernadette had managed to make a "small private chapel" out of her veil when she first came to the Motherhouse. Now from this letter which she wrote to a Sister at Lourdes in the spring of 1876, we learn that she had managed to make a chapel out of her bed.

She was there nearly all the time, for her asthma had grown constantly worse and she had been beset by other ills as well, among them a tumor on her knee. But she was not restless or discontented. In spite of the difficulty which she had with breathing and the suffering which this

107

brought with it, she was one of those resourceful persons who know instinctively how to adapt themselves to a sickroom, to maintain its cheerfulness, and to live there a life which is contented and complete over indefinite periods of time. Even the reproach of a Sister who felt she was probably not as sick as she seemed lacked a sting sharp enough to penetrate her serenity.

"What are you doing there in bed, you lazy little thing?"

"I am doing my stint."

"What stint?"

"Why, the stint of learning to be an invalid!"

Her comparison to a chapel was apt. The narrow bed where she lay, with its snowy sheets and its soft linen curtain, had much of the sanctity and seclusion of such a spot. The "stint" which she did there was not without a quality of worship.

Her state of mind had a great deal to do with her attitude. She had recaptured this when the wounds of war began to heal and when, over the rough road that led to national recovery, the radiance of fresh purpose and fresh faith had begun to glow. Her country was at peace again, and so was she. Her conscience was as clear as crystal. On one of the rare occasions when she was able to leave the infirmary, she went to the Great Hall of the Novitiate to listen to a sermon given by the chaplain. As she started back to bed, she told the companion upon whom she was leaning that the discourse had made her extremely happy.

"But why? The preacher talked about sin!"

"Yes, but didn't you hear what he said?"

"I don't know what you mean!"

"He said that no one really sinned without having

108

wished to do so. I cannot remember that I have ever wished to sin in my whole life, no, not once. Therefore, apparently I haven't. That is what makes me so happy!"

She was certainly very happy. And she made others happy also. On the days when she was well enough, she rose at the recreation hour and went into the adjoining ward, taking with her great good cheer. The novices who were confined there still loved to talk, as old women, about her brief visits, about the merry stories she told and the sidesplitting imitations she gave of their physician, Dr. Robert, a kindly old man whose quaint mannerisms made him a logical target for the young Sisters' gentle mockery. When the end of the recreation hour brought Bernadette's call to a close, she grew grave again and took her leave of her fellow invalids with careful courtesy. But meanwhile she had done something surprising to the sickroom. Its gloom had been lightened, its tedium whiled away, its emptiness filled.

Another reason for her happiness, besides her peace of mind and her unquenchable gaiety, was her industry. She did not lie still, thinking how ill she felt. She kept her hands and her thoughts both busy. The most beautiful lacework which she ever achieved she did at this time.(31) She also wrote a great many letters. It is unfortunate that not more of them have been preserved, but she always implored her correspondents to destroy what she wrote, because of her reluctance to risk having her letters seen by anyone except the person for whom they were primarily intended. It is unfortunate, as far as posterity is concerned, that her wishes were for the most part scrupulously observed. But in some instances they were disre-

109

garded, and it is difficult for us to regret this, for it reveals a side of her character which otherwise might have remained undisclosed.

The letters she wrote to her family were especially wise and tender. Her mother and father had both died and, with their passing, the solicitude of the elder sister, responsible for the rest of the brood, which she had felt so keenly when she was a little girl, began to deepen again. Now that she knew the days of her own surveillance were numbered, the loving-kindness which swelled her heart flowed from her pen also.

"Cousin Nicolau says in his last letter that you are expecting your discharge this year," she wrote to her brother Jean, who was completing his military service. "Tell me what you are thinking of doing next. You know that though I am far away, I feel the same interest as if I were near you. So if I ask this question, please realize, my dear, that it is not through curiosity. Now that we have lost our parents, it seems that it is my duty, as the eldest, to watch over you and the others. It is superfluous for me to say how much you all mean to me.

"I confess that at this moment I am greatly preoccupied with your future and careers. I pray every day to Our Saviour and to the Blessed Virgin to clarify the way for you. I venture to suggest that before everything you should be constant in your Christian duty. In that way you will find strength and light in all your troubles and difficulties. I know that soldiers must suffer a great deal in silence. If every morning they would say this short prayer, 'Lord, today I will do my best, my very best, and accept my lot for love of Thee!' how much eternal grace they would store up for themselves! A soldier who did

110

this, and who also—insofar as his military duties would permit—was also constant in all Christian duties, would have as much merit as a priest."

To "petit Pierre,"(32) the Benjamin of the family, who held in her heart the favored place so often reserved for the youngest child, she wrote still more tenderly.

"It gave me complete satisfaction, my dear little brother, to learn that you had made your First Communion on the ninth of June. It goes without saying that henceforth you should strive to make your heart, your mind, and your soul the abode of God. Pray that He Himself may prepare this dwelling place, so that nothing may be lacking on His arrival."

Pierre was having trouble with his teachers, the Pères de Garaison, at the time. There was some question that he might leave school, and his brother-in-law, Joseph, the husband of Marie Toinette,(33) had offered to set him up in some sort of little shop, if he did so. Bernadette was deeply distressed. "I am surprised at what you tell me," she wrote to Pierre himself. "Go find Monsieur le Curé, confide all your troubles to him, and do what he tells you. This is the only advice I shall give you on the subject, and it is wholly in your interest."

To other members of the family she wrote more fully and forcefully. She made no effort to conceal the fact that she was not at all pleased with the idea of the shop, that she was indeed decidedly opposed to it. *"Cela ne convient pas"* ("It is not suitable"), she said uncomprisingly. "I want Pierre to stay where the Bishop of Tarbes wished him left to be educated. . . . Nothing must interfere with this dear child's studies. I know that the Fathers are very well pleased with him. Don't listen to unsound advice. I am the eldest, I have a right to watch over my little brother."

She would have rejoiced to feel that this little brother whom she loved so dearly had a vocation for the priesthood. But she viewed the situation sanely and without sentimentality.

"If you really think you have no calling for a religious life," she wrote him, "I strongly advise you to begin thinking about learning a trade. If you are fond of manual labor, you could always earn a living. Think it over carefully and ask God's guidance. Not for the world would I have you become a priest merely to get a position. I would rather you were a ragpicker."

Besides writing letters, Sister Marie Bernard also wrote in a tiny notebook,(34) where she recorded her own thoughts, her own ideals and her own prayers. On the flyleaf it bears the inscription:

Diary dedicated to the Queen of Heaven, in the month of May, 1866.

Underneath are the words:

How happy was my heart, beneficent Mother, when I had the privilege of contemplating your presence! How I love to recall the blissful moments spent beneath your kind and compassionate gaze!

A prayer for the virtue of humility follows this dedication. Then comes the statement: "You know that it will be my joy to consecrate myself to religion, in order the better to serve you and your Divine Son. I pray you to remove every obstacle that there might be in my path, which may prevent me from attaining this end."

It was during her last days at Lourdes that she had written with such faith and fervor, when she was standing on the threshold of her novitiate. In the years that had elapsed since then, the faith had never faltered, the fervor had never cooled. There are many entries which reveal the conscientiousness with which she prepared for annual retreats and undertook self-examination. "I must be sure to do whatever seems hardest" is the notation inscribed against the records of four successive months. She made ready for Communion with the same solicitude. "The proper preparation lies in meditation," she stated with her usual clarity, "and I am not capable of meditating well." Like most great mystics, she saw everything clearly except her own rare gifts.

Opening the precious little volume at random, and leafing it through, we do not find a single passage that shows doubt or discontent amid the many that bespeak docility.

"Not my will, dear Mother, but yours, which is always the same as that of Jesus."

"Lord, give me, I pray Thee, the love of my cross."

"Let me begin here on earth to glorify the Saviour by my perpetual homage of complete submission."

As the days grew harder and the nights more hideous, a cry of desperation sometimes rang out. No one in the Motherhouse heard it. But God must have heard it. And we find it still recorded in the delicate handwriting that betrays no trace of the writer's anguish.

"Mary, compassionate Mother, here is your child who

113

can do no more. Look down upon her need and her distress. Have pity on her. Grant that some day she may be in Heaven with you."

"O holy Mother of Jesus, you have seen and felt the supreme desolation of your own Son. Help me in my hour of agony."

"Heaven is my home. I will do everything I can to reach it. There I shall find my beneficent Mother in all her radiance and, with her, I shall glorify God in the blessedness of perfect peace."

The Beautiful Lady had promised her that Heaven should be her home; this she asserted confidently and as confidently believed. "But," she added, "on the condition that I shall go straight along the road that leads there and do all I can to deserve it. They say that sometimes even saints have not been willing to do this. It will not be so in my case."

She spoke the truth. It was not so in her case. But though her spirit was willing, her flesh was indeed very weak. She was grateful for everything that made the way easier, and the offerings which came to her bedside took many different forms. A Sister, who knew how much she loved flowers, gathered some violets which had bloomed almost miraculously in the autumnal sunshine that warmed the kitchen wall and sent them to her with the message that they were a present to her on her own feast day, since it was the festival of All Saints and she was one of these. The next day the thoughtful giver received a return compliment. "If it is my feast day, then it is yours also," was the message Bernadette sent to her. "Please accept half of my little cakes, and without scruples. I have permission to offer them to you."

No doubt she held the violets for a long time in her fragile fingers, feeling their frostiness, smelling their fragrance. Once it had been her habit surreptitiously to rearrange the bouquets which were given her when they were stiff or ill assorted; but that was all over now and, in any case, the lovely late-blooming violets met her every standard of delicacy and taste.

For a long time she had yearned for a large crucifix on her bed. Such an ornament was highly suitable for "a little white chapel," and eventually the Superior of Cahors sent her one. "I do not know how to thank you enough," she wrote him happily. "I cried for joy when I took it in my hands. I have permission to keep it. I am more contented with this Christ on my bed than a queen could be on her throne."

Besides finding joy in the crucifix, she loved to look at the statue of the Lady of Lourdes which surmounted the mantelpiece. It was almost the only statue of the Virgin which wholly pleased her; most sculptors, she felt, had failed to invest the Beautiful Lady with all the grace and glory so essentially hers. When Bernadette had first seen the image on which the famous sculptor Fabisch had lavished all his skill for months, she had regarded it thoughtfully and then she had said, "Oh, it is very beautiful, but it is not she. There is all the difference between this and the original that exists between earth and heaven." Later, when she had gone to see an altarpiece, installed with pride at the Cathedral of Nevers, she had almost cried in disappointment and chagrin. "Oh! how plain they have made her, my Beautiful Lady!" she had exclaimed. But she loved the little statue on the mantelpiece. While she was still working in the infirmary her-

115

self, before this mortal illness had seized her in its clutch, she had been surprised, more than once, in the act of lifting it from its shelf and kissing the hem of its robe, while she was busy about her dusting. Now she could not do that any more. But she worshiped it with her eyes, as she lay in her little white chapel.

She continued to receive Communion regularly, and one of her companions in the infirmary, Sister Marcelline Durand, has left us a touching account of the way she did it: "She made a little ceremony of getting ready, and often I was in charge of this. We raised her on her bed and arranged her headdress as if she were up and about. Then we left her, at her request, in the most complete silence. After Holy Communion, she replaced on her bed the little napkin on which her clasped hands rested all the time the action of grace lasted, which was about a quarter of an hour. During this time, we were very careful to avoid making the least sound."

Her little white chapel was well suited for such a ceremony. No wonder she found joy in it after her wakeful nights of suffering. For it was the nights which were the hardest. She could not sew then, or write "petit Pierre" or gaze at the Beautiful Lady. Darkness engulfed her, and this did not always seem friendly; her cough was worse when it came. A novice was detailed to sleep in the bed beside hers, but if the young girl watched, instead of resting, Sister Marie Bernard always knew it. "Please do not send Sœur Saint Michel to me again," she said to the Mother General. "She did not close her eyes. I cannot bear to feel that she is losing sleep on account of me."

"I cannot imagine how she knew I did not sleep," Sœur

Saint Michel told me. She was a very old lady, one of the oldest at the Motherhouse in Nevers, when I first went there.(34-A) But, as she talked, the years faded away. She took me back to that hushed room with tall windows, where the Lady of Lourdes looked down from the mantelpiece; the white-curtained beds were ranged side by side on the clean bare floor, a small straight-backed chair beside each, and the only sound that penetrated the stillness was Sister Marie Bernard's stifled cough.

"I thought I had not moved a muscle all night," Sœur Saint Michel went on. "I was so careful not to disturb her, so eager to be allowed to stay with her, right along. It was a privilege which all of us sought eagerly. I hoped she would ask me to do something for her, to get her a drink, to shift her pillow. But she did not speak to me at all— not then, I mean. Of course, at other times she often did. And the very next day, our dear Mother said to me, 'Sœur Saint Michel, you will be replaced in the infirmary tonight. Sœur Marie Bernard says you did not sleep at all.' It was true, so what could I do? But after all, Madame, I watched beside her once."

The fine old face, smooth and white as ancient ivory, was illumined as she talked. It was very quiet in the imposing parlor of the Motherhouse at Nevers. Even the big clock on the wall stopped ticking. The curtains were drawn to shut out the sun which otherwise would have streamed in, but the tempered light was mellow all the same. At the foot of every chair there was a small round mat, soft against the polished floor, on which to put one's feet. The Mother General had arranged that there should be no interruption, no disturbance, while Sœur Saint

117

Michel told the story of what she had seen with her own eyes and heard with her own ears—a story which no printed page can reproduce in all its poignancy.

"By and by, she was very weak, she could not hold her crucifix herself. It was placed against her breast so that she could feel it there. Sometimes she could breathe better when she sat up for a little while, on the edge of her bed or in an armchair. Someone supported her, someone helped her to rise. She was sitting in her armchair on Easter Wednesday, during the afternoon. The chaplain had been called. He was praying beside her, and she prayed too. Her hands fluttered a little across her breast, but her face was calm and her voice was very clear. She said, 'Lord, I love Thee with all my heart and with all my strength and with all my soul.' She must have suddenly felt stronger than she had in a long time, for she was able to take the crucifix in her own hands, to hold it, to kiss it. But she was thirsty. She said so, and the Sister who was standing near her gave her something to drink. She begged pardon for being so much trouble. Trouble! She was never any trouble to anyone! She made the sign of the cross again, in an exalted way. She always seemed exalted when she did that. And then she murmured, 'Holy Mary, Mother of God, pray for us, miserable sinners—miserable sinners. . . .'"

She never added, "Now and in the hour of our death. Amen." For in this case the two were the same. Sœur Saint Michel's story was finished. Sœur Marie Bernard had died with the prayer she loved on her lips. At Eastertime, when all the world was repeating the everlasting promise, "I am the resurrection and the life; he who
118

believes in me, even if he die, shall live; and whoever lives and believes in me, shall never die."

I wonder, in those last moments, if Sœur Marie Bernard heard that promise, echoing down through the ages. I hope so. I believe so. For only the Sister had died. The Saint could not perish.

PART THREE

The Saint

✿ ELEVEN ✿

In the chapel of the Motherhouse at Nevers there is a coffin of gold and glass. It is richly decorated with doves and lilies, inscribed with significant dates and memorable quotations, and surmounted by the jeweled initials N. D. L. Rays of azure light, streaming from the windows of the vaulted arch behind it, slant across it. The tapers in the tall candelabra standing on either side of it flicker gently. Above the altar which it fronts, a snowy statue of the Virgin glows with soft radiance, and to the left and right of this are frescoed angels. Close by, a nun with a bent head kneels at a small *prie-dieu*, her black habit somber against her luminous surroundings.

Her immobility is complete. Indeed, the shining statue rising between the arches seems less fixed a figure than she does, because, like so many inspired representations of the Virgin, it suggests ascent. The stillness of the nun is comparable only to that of the slender form encased in the coffin of glass and gold.

This also is clad in a black habit. The tranquil face, perfectly at peace, is framed with a white wimple, from which two white tabs descend over the breast. The grace-

123

ful head rests lightly on a lace-covered pillow. With the same lightness, the fingers of the small clasped hands are interlaced with a rosary. The folds of the dress flow down, full and free, over the feet, and these do not come close to the foot of the coffin, because this figure is short as well as slight. It is a childlike figure, and a child might lie like this, quietly in bed, when the house was hushed for the night.

But it is not the figure of a child. It is the figure of a Saint.

She was not always buried here. In the olden days, if you wished to see her first resting place, you skirted the Motherhouse to the left, past the old stable, where quaint carriages were still enclosed, and the old *lavoir*, where washing was still done. Then you turned again, this time into the kitchen garden, which lay on the sunny slope back of the Motherhouse, so that you looked up toward this as you trod the neat paths and saw the arches of its cloister beyond great, glossy trees and its wide wings stretching out solidly and spaciously on either side. There were fruit trees as well as vegetables in the garden, for it served as an orchard also, and in the autumn the boughs of these were heavy with peaches and apples, glossy in the sunshine, while melons lay like golden balls among their vines. With the apparent artlessness which represents extreme delicacy of taste, the lifelike figures of a shepherdess surrounded by her flock and guarded by her dog had been placed on a grassy plot at the back of this garden. And it was here, too, that a small stone chapel stood, completely sheathed inside with the rectangular tablets made of marble and inscribed with gold lettering, which

124

the French characteristically employ to memorialize their gratitude for special favors and benefits received. There were three small stained glass windows back of the altar: St. Joseph in the center, with his lilies and his Foster Son; St. Augustine and his *De Civitate Dei* at the left, St. Dominic, the "Apostle of the Rosary," with his own insignia at the right—all benign of presence, as befitted so serene a spot. But it was Our Lady of Lourdes, robed in white and girdled in blue, who surmounted the altar itself, which was even more fitting still. For midway down the pavement of black and white marble was embedded a slab which bore the significant inscription:

ICI REPOSE

DANS LA PAIX DU SEIGNEUR

BERNADETTE SOUBIROUS

HONORÉE A LOURDES, EN 1858

DE PLUSIERS APPARITIONS DE LA

TRÈS SAINTE VIERGE:

EN RELIGION

SOEUR MARIE-BERNARD

DÉCÉDÉE A NEVERS

A LA MAISON-MÈRE

DES SOEURS DE LA CHARITÉ

LE 16 AVRIL, 1879,

DANS LA 36me ANNÉE DE SON AGE

ET LA 12me DE SA PROFESSION RELIGIEUSE.(35)

And as epitaph, these words of the Prophet which summed up the wish often expressed by the Saint that she be buried at Nevers in the midst of her Sisters:

This was followed by the wish of the Church for those
of her children whose time of exile has ended:

REQUIESCAT IN PACE.

The whole was surmounted by the device, DEUS
CHARITAS EST, above which gleams the cross.

As I have said, this is the way it was in the old days.
Instead, I might have said, "This was the way it was when
I first saw it and as I shall always want to think of it."
But then, I should have been obliged to add, "It is not
that way any longer. That is not the way I last saw it."

We have noted that "The alien army, which had been
sweeping over the countryside, leaving death and disaster
in its wake, never succeeded in entering Nevers." But
that was in 1870. In 1944, an alien army did succeed in
doing so; and though it was an army of deliverance, still
it left death and destruction in its wake. The Motherhouse escaped and so did all its occupants. But seventeen
bombs fell in and about that peaceful and productive
garden. One of them killed the faithful gardener, his wife
and his son. Another destroyed the rustic shelter and most
of the sculptured sheep. Still another reduced the Gothic
arches of the little chapel to ruins, its stained glass windows to fragments and its black and white marble pavement to rubble. But by some strange chance—or was it
really chance after all?—when the tragic debris had been
126

cleared away, the slab marking Sister Marie Bernard's first resting place was completely undamaged!

It was four days after her death that she was buried in the beautiful little votive chapel of which that solitary stone slab, with its startlingly clear inscription, is all that remains. Usually, a funeral was not delayed so long. But the circumstances had been extraordinary. The news that she had breathed her last was hardly divulged to the community when the whole town seemed to know it; she had no sooner been laid in state than multitudes began surging toward the chapel. It was as if all the world wished to see the Sister whose own wish had been to remain unseen by the world. But it was not idle curiosity which prompted the crowds to come. It was veneration. The four Sisters who kept vigil beside the bier were constantly besought to place, ever so fleetingly, small objects against some part of the quiet form that rested so tranquilly between its guardians. Some of these were objects of piety, but by no means all. Workmen brought their tools, seamstresses their scissors, to be blessed; afterward, there would always be something consecrated in the use of these, or so their owners believed, and how could the Sisters put a blight upon their faith? The tools and the scissors were handled as reverently as the medals and the crosses.

Outside the enclosure of the Motherhouse, emotion was almost as great as it was within. And there was a new word on the people's lips as they spoke. A poor woman, who had not been able to get into the chapel because of the crowd, met one of the Sisters in the park which stretches out near by in the unadorned green expanse characteristic of a New England common rather than that of a French public garden.

127

"What time will the cortege pass by on its way to the cemetery?" she asked timidly. "I should like to see that at least."

"We are not taking Sister Marie Bernard to the cemetery. We are keeping her ourselves," the Sister answered, kindly but proudly.

"Oh! I am very glad. Of course it is not for me to say, Sister. But I do not believe she was merely a Christian lady. I believe she was a Saint."

In the bustling railroad station echoed the same word that had been heard in the peaceful park. Every incoming train disgorged endless passengers. They all had the same reason to give for their arrival in Nevers. They had come to attend the funeral of a Saint.

The new word was not always pronounced reverently; that is, not at first. Two young men, sauntering through the streets in the gay and easy manner of their kind, said to each other, "Come, let us go and have a look at this Saint, like everyone else!" They went into the chapel jauntily. But they stayed there a long time, and none of those surrounding the bier was more respectful than they. When they left the chapel they parted gravely, without speaking to each other, and went their separate ways.

The Sisters who were keeping vigil did not form the new word with their lips. But they felt the force of it and the meaning of it in their hearts. It was not only the poor and ignorant who came pressing around them. The commandant of the regiment entered and, kneeling down, prayed as he never had before. The clergy appeared from far and wide. Abbé Pomian was there, the priest who had told the little shepherdess from Bartrès that if she would come to Lourdes he would prepare her for her First Communion. He passed proudly along, amid twenty-four prelates, and though there were those who outranked him, there was none who held so symbolic a place—not even the Bishop of Nevers, Monseigneur Lelong, who preached to the text, taken from Tobias: "It is good to hide the secret of the king. But it is honorable to reveal and bear witness to the works of God."

The terrace was filled and all the great courtyards, as the body was borne from the chapel of the congregation through the garden to the votive chapel of St. Joseph which is enshrined there. A garden tomb at Eastertime. Did anyone speak of its significance, or think of it?

I do not know. Perhaps all thoughts were preoccupied. For many persons were absorbed by the phenomenon which they saw. It was now four days since Sister Bernard had died, and the congregation had followed its invariable custom in regard to its dead: no artificial means had been used to prevent the return of "dust to dust, ashes to ashes." And yet the Sister, who was not yet hidden—since all had begged to look at her once more—still lay relaxed, as if she were only sleeping. Her form had no rigidity, her face no pallor. Even her finger tips were rosy. The Archpriest of the cathedral, Abbé Greuzard, unable to suppress his surprise, called upon the Commissioner of Police, who was also present, to bear witness to her condition. Amazed in his turn, the Commissioner did so. An affidavit was put in the coffin, which was reverently placed at the foot of the altar. The dignitaries who had attended the funeral dispersed. Late in the afternoon, the members of the Community Council, and a few other notables, returned to the chapel to recite the rosary. The Superior of the Fathers of Lourdes, Father Sempe, paraphrased the Mysteries. Then at last the coffin was closed.

It was not placed immediately in the tomb, as this was not yet in complete readiness to receive it. Therefore it remained for some days longer at the altar steps and many still came to pray beside it. There was a little boy whose mother brought him there and whose hands were full of daisies when he entered. While the woman prayed, the child wove a wreath; when she arose from her knees, he placed this on the coffin. It lay there, soft and snowy, a child's freewill offering, until the coffin was lowered into the tomb.

Thirty years later the stone was lifted again, the coffin raised and unsealed. When it was opened, the stupefied authorities saw that it contained the slender figure, still lovely and unravished, of Sister Marie Bernard.

✹ TWELVE ✹

AGAIN I am going to resort to the testimony of an eye-witness, instead of to a printed page, in order to describe what happened next. It was not Sœur Saint Michel who told me about this. It was Sœur Marie Marguerite, a younger Sister—though she was an old lady when she talked to me(36-a)—who had not known Sœur Marie Bernard in the flesh, as the other had done, but who was present both times that her body was exhumed. Again, the great lofty parlor of the Motherhouse was very still as I listened to an incomparable tale, on a sunny autumn afternoon, while, all unheard outside, the first troops mobilized for another war went marching past. I cannot promise that I can repeat, word for word, everything that was said. But to the best of my knowledge and under-standing, the essentials of the conversation which took place were like this:

"But Sister, why was it necessary to open the coffin?"

"Because, madame, it was obligatory that the mortal remains of Sister Marie Bernard should be authenticated before the first canonical steps could be taken which would eventually lead to her beatification and canoniza-

131

tion. Such measures are always taken, in cases of this kind, to guard against fraud."

"I see. And was the entire congregation present in the chapel of St. Joseph?"

"Certainly, madame. The entire congregation and the foremost ecclesiastical and civil authorities of Nevers. That was also essential."

"And you were standing close enough to the coffin to see it when it was opened?"

"Oh, yes, madame. That is one of my most sacred memories. I was so close that I could kiss the feet of the Saint. And I was allowed to do so."

"You are perfectly sure that her body had not been embalmed when she died?"

"Oh, as to that, madame—" For the first time there was the least suggestion of reproach, of injured pride, in the quiet, cultured voice. "There had been no embalmment," Sœur Marie Marguerite continued with dignity. *"Ce n'est pas de nos usages*—it is not our custom. But after thirty years, the face and form of Sister Marie Bernard were exactly as those who had been her close companions thirty years earlier best loved to remember her. When they and the assisting authorities recovered from their astonishment, and the necessary affidavits had been taken, the body was borne tenderly away from the chapel. It was not even rigid. All clothing was removed from it by the Sisters, even to the chemise. These garments were preserved for relics. And since, as you can see for yourself, madame, our habits are very full, it was possible to make a great many small relics out of the garments in which Sister Marie Bernard had first been buried.

"After the removal of the clothing, the body was bathed

132

à grand eau—with a great deal of water. That was a mistake. The body of one long dead should never be cleansed in this way. But the Sisters did not think of that at the time. They thought only of consigning her, in complete freshness, to her new tomb, and of the great benefits which the water in which she had been bathed would bestow upon all who were fortunate enough to secure a few drops preserved in a small vial."

"So after this she was put in a new tomb?"

"Not in a new tomb, madame, that is not quite correct. I should have said in a new coffin. Two repositories had already been prepared, at the time of the exhumation: a small casket, in case only ossicles were found, and a full-sized coffin, in case there were still the semblance of a body—that there would be more than this, no one had ever dreamed! After the ceremonies which I have described to you, the body of the Saint was reverently laid in a new coffin and this was replaced in the same tomb as before, under the pavement in the chapel of St. Joseph. It remained there for ten years more."

"And then?"

"Then it was exhumed again, madame, at the end of the Process. In the meantime, His Holiness Pope Pius X had signed the decree for the introduction of the Cause of the Servant of God(36) and had conferred upon her the title of Venerable. The World War delayed the next proceedings. It was not until September, 1917, that Monseigneur Chatelus, then Bishop of Nevers, opened the Apostolic Process, which held over two hundred hearings."

"And what happened at the time of the second exhumation, Sister?"

"The body of the Saint was still beautifully preserved, but the face was found slightly discolored. This was because it had been washed. That should never have been done, as I said. So it was decided to cover the face and hands with a light coating of wax. I was reconciled to having the face so covered. But I should have liked to have had the hands left exactly as they were—her dear little brown hands!"

I could see them: the dear little brown hands that had been so busy and so willing, that had been folded in resignation and raised in prayer. I was not sorry that Sister Marie Marguerite paused for a moment before she went on. I knew she was thinking about them, too, and that our thoughts were much the same.

"Eh bien—a very celebrated worker in wax was entrusted with the task, and he trembled before it. He had often placed such a coating over the faces of the dead. But only of the newly dead. Now he was summoned to cover the face of a woman dead for forty years."

Sister Marie Marguerite paused again and for the second time corrected herself. "That is to say, of a Saint. Therefore he had no trouble. He accomplished his task easily and well. And after that, Sister Marie Bernard was not entombed again beneath the pavement of St. Joseph's chapel. She was enshrined as you have seen her, madame, in glass and gold."

This brings me back to the place where I myself started to tell you about the coffin of glass and gold, and as far as I am concerned, Sister Marie Marguerite's account of what happened is both adequate and convincing. But lest you should not feel the same way about it, lest you should prefer the record of the printed page to the word of mouth indirectly given, let me quote from the book written by the Reverend Mother Marie Thérèse Bordenave of the Sisters of Nevers, which I myself have found as helpful in interpreting the vocation of Sister Marie Bernard as I found J. B. Estrade's book helpful in interpreting the apparitions and which is universally regarded as a leading authority.

"Already, at the time of her death," writes Mother Marie Thérèse, "the Curé of Lourdes, announcing to his parishioners a service for the repose of the soul of Sister Marie Bernard, said to them, 'In praying for Bernadette, we also invoke her, for she had all the characteristics of predestined souls: that is to say, virginity, humility and long-suffering. Moreover her every quality had been illumined by rays of glory from the Immaculate Mother.' . . .

"Her reputation for saintliness, which increased all the time, the ever-mounting number of pilgrims to her tomb, the abundance of divine favors which the faithful all over the world attributed to her intercession—these were the adequate motives which moved the Reverend Mother General of the Sisters of Nevers, encouraged by the Bishop of Nevers, to occupy herself actively with the cause for Beatification. Indeed it was really a response to the desire of the Catholic universe.

"The Sacred Heart had placed on the episcopal throne of Nevers Monseigneur Gauthey, one of Sister Marie Bernard's most ardent apostles. For him was reserved the joy—indeed why should we not say the glory?—of opening the long proceedings which were crowned on December 8, 1933, by the canonization of the Immaculate Virgin's confidante.

"The first session of the Ordinary Process, that is to say the constitution of the Ecclesiastical Court charged with gathering witnesses on the life, virtues, reputation for saintliness and miracles of the Servant of God took place on August 20, 1908, in the chapel of the Motherhouse.

"The distinguished Prelate, ably seconded by the other eminent personages, of whom the Ecclesiastical Court was made up, carried on the investigations with such zeal and skill that in October 1909 the Process was handed in to the Sacred Congregation of Rites. There had been one hundred and thirty-three sessions.

"On September 22 of this same year, that is to say thirty years after the burial of Sister Marie Bernard in St. Joseph's chapel, the verification of her mortal remains took place according to canonical form.

"The exhumation took place in the presence of Monseigneur Gauthey and the members of the Court of the Cause of the Servant of God, after the observance of all legal requirements and in the presence of two doctors. The coffin was removed from the tomb by workmen who had been especially sworn in for the undertaking and carried to a pavilion adjacent to St. Joseph's. There it was opened. No odor escaped when the leaden vault was broken. The Servant of God was revealed fully clothed in her habit. Her face, her hands, and her forearms alone were uncovered; they were all a clear white. Her lips were slightly parted, showing her teeth; her closed eyes were somewhat sunken. Her hands, crossed upon her breast, were perfectly preserved, even to her nails; they were interlaced with a rosary which had become rusty. A crucifix, covered with verdigris, lay on her breast. Her veins still stood out slightly from her forearms.(36-A)

136

"The Mother General of the Sisters of Nevers and the members of her congregation removed the damp garments and the sawdust mingled with charcoal which surrounded the body. They could swear, and so could the doctors, that it was emaciated but whole and without any signs of corruption.

"The left side of the body, from the hip down, was slightly raised above the right side. The left knee was smaller than the right.(37) The head and the hands were slightly inclined to the left, so that Sister Marie Bernarde's attitude recalled—as the venerable Prelate had remarked at the time of the exhumation—that of the earliest virgin martyrs found in the catacombs.

"The Sisters washed the body. After having clothed it anew in a habit, they replaced it, with tender care, in the new coffin, sheathed with zinc and lined with white satin. The head lay on a white satin cushion, embroidered with the initials of Notre Dame de Lourdes. The same initials were carved on the coffin. An affidavit of the examination and the identification of the body, together with the original affidavit of the burial, were placed beside the body in a crystal flagon.

"This double coffin, soldered, screwed down, and sealed with the episcopal crest, was replaced in the tomb. . . .

"The second exhumation took place at the end of the Process on April 3, 1919. The body of the Venerable(38) was found in the same state of preservation as ten years earlier.

"On the eighteenth of November 1923, His Holiness Pius XI published the 'Decree on the Heroism of the Virtues of the Venerable Sister Marie Bernard Soubirous.' . . . 'This ceremony, so important and so lovely,'

Monseigneur Chateles tells us, 'took place in the Ducal Hall in the presence of the Supreme Pontiff and His court, before the entire French Colony in Rome.' . . . 'There is no doubt,' the Pontiff said, 'that here we are in the presence of saintliness in the exact and precise sense of the word. Indeed, when we consider the life of Bernadette as it has emerged from all phases of the Process . . . it can be summed up in three words: *Bernadette was* FAITHFUL *to her mission, she was* HUMBLE *in her glory, and she was* STRONG *when she was put to the test.'*

"In concluding this address, the Holy Father expressed the hope that Bernadette Soubirous might soon be elevated to the glory conferred by the Church on its Saints. This hope was realized: On June 2, 1925, in the Consistory, was read the decree *de tuto* for the Beatification of Sister Marie Bernard, at the same time as similar decrees concerning the Martyrs of Canada, the Martyrs of Korea, and the Reverend Father Eymard. . . .

"It was the happy privilege of the Motherhouse to open the solemn ceremonies in honor of the Beatified. On the third of August, Bernadette, intact in her precious and symbolic reliquary, made her triumphant re-entry into that chapel where, forty-six years earlier, her mortal remains, laid in state immediately after her death, had already attracted such multitudes. She returned to it in all the majesty of a queen, triumphantly borne through a crowd so great that the vast courts of the convent could not contain it."

So here is another version of the story I started to tell you about the coffin of glass and gold. The Saint who lies within it resembles, in very truth, those early Virgins entombed in the catacombs; the same grace enfolds her form, the same quietude is in her face. I am glad that in the annals of Nevers, Sister Marie Bernard was compared to Cecilia and Agnes and the other maiden martyrs, who, for centuries, have been numbered among the blessed. The comparison is appropriate and beautiful. But I am gladder still that the writer of these same annals thought of comparing her to a queen in her majesty when she returned in triumph to the chapel where once, in her humility, she had hidden her face behind her veil. For is it not also written, elsewhere, that at the end the first shall be last and the last first?

❂ THIRTEEN ❂

THERE are many who have told the story of Lourdes and its wonders better than I could tell it. So why should I attempt the task? In any event that was not the story I started out to tell. I have only tried to tell the story of a shepherdess who eventually became a Sister and who is now a Saint for all time.

I have almost finished what I meant to say, or thought I could. But I may perhaps remind the reader—lest his memory for dates be no better than mine—that it is over eighty years now since the great Basilica of Notre Dame was consecrated at Lourdes. I doubt if he needs a reminder that in all the years since then, and for many years before that, pilgrims in endless processions have turned their faces toward it. From every country in the world they have come, carrying flaming torches through the night, kneeling with extended arms when rain fell all around them, bending their heads to shield their blinded eyes from the glory of the midday sun; all sorts and conditions of men: the lame, the halt and the blind; the sorrowful and the sinful, the rich and the poor. They have bathed in the fountain and drunk of it. They have been

140

healed and comforted. They have sought and found. They have asked and they have received.

But the supreme service which Bernadette Soubirous rendered mankind is not found, primarily, in the field of physical healing, or even in the realm of mental assuagement and encouragement which, we should never forget, also holds a paramount place in the scheme of things at Lourdes. She performed a higher service than that. As Pius X expressed it, "She brought the world into the closest possible touch with the mystery of Christ the Saviour. That is the great thing she did, the greatest thing that anyone can do."

And how did she do it? You must decide that point, of course, for yourself, provided you are ready and willing to concede that she did do it. But I have my own belief in the matter, the belief to which I have tried to bear witness on every page of this book. Now that the book is nearly finished, however, perhaps I should define it in greater detail, lest I should have failed, through lack of skill, to make my meaning clear.

I believe that she brought the world close to Christ the Saviour because her self-respect was such that nothing could undermine it. She lived in a hovel, she went hungry, she dwelt for years in ignorance. Yet somehow she always found the way to be tidy, the strength to refuse alms, and the ingenuity to substitute sound sense for profound learning. Self-respect is always the first basic step toward respect for God. Having achieved the one, the other followed, normally and unsensationally. It represents logical and ordered progress. It is wholly natural.

I believe that she brought the world close to Christ the Saviour because she was cheerful and industrious. Moros-

141

ity and idleness are both archenemies of consecrated living. The great Teresa of Ávila was wont to say, "May God preserve us from frowning saints!" She would have enjoyed Bernadette and approved of her. There is a still older saying to the effect that Satan finds some mischief still for idle hands to do. But God has a way of helping busy hands to do His work as well as their own. Such hands build temples which reach upward to the sky, and Heaven comes closer and ever closer as the towers ascend. It is inevitable.

I believe Bernadette brought the world close to Christ the Saviour because she had such a rare gift for distinguishing the material from the spiritual and for weighing the comparative merits of the two. She knew how to render unto Caesar the things which are Caesar's and unto God the things which are God's. Anyone who can see clearly enough to do that has gone a long way toward clarifying mysteries for others. An accurate sense of values is indispensable for the soul groping through clouds of doubt and distrust. It is so easy to make obstacles of nonessentials. She swept these all away in the course of her own search for Christ and left an open road behind her.

I believe Bernadette has brought the world close to Christ the Saviour because she was so composed. We live in the midst of confusion and chaos, and it is very hard not to be drawn into the whirlpool of this. The more we move around in senseless or vicious circles, the harder it is to achieve and maintain that physical repose, that mental clarity and that spiritual serenity which are indivisibly essential for wholesome living, creative thought and righteous standards. I doubt very much if Bernadette ever heard of a hymn which was a great favorite among the
142

early American missionaries to the Near East, and which originally formed part of John Greenleaf Whittier's great poem, "The Brewing of Soma." But she might well have written a similar song herself; in any event, she expressed and exemplified this one in a thousand different ways. It reads, in part, like this:

> "Dear Lord and Saviour of mankind,
>   Forgive our feverish ways,
>   Restore us to our rightful mind,
>   In firmer faith our service find,
>   In deeper reverence, praise.
>
> "Drop Thy sweet dews of quietness,
>   Till all our strivings cease.
>   Take from our souls the strain and stress
>   And let our ordered lives confess
>   The beauty of Thy peace."

I believe she brought the world close to Christ the Saviour because she had so much true Christian resignation. It is a very rare quality, as distinct from the characteristic of abject groveling as it is from the characteristic of headstrong rebellion. Most of us find it as hard to be dignified in submission as we do to be tranquil under opposition. She gave grace to patience and distinction to docility. It was by no means the least of her services to mankind.

I believe that she brought the world close to Christ the Saviour because she was so sincere. If she had ever succumbed to the temptation of embellishing or embroidering her story of the apparitions, if she had claimed to see or hear the veriest trifle more than she actually had seen or heard, she would have been caught in her own toils. She would have been distrusted and disgraced, and rightly so. It is to her sincerity, more than to any other one quality of hers, that we owe the existence of the mighty and miraculous Lourdes of today and the universal acceptance of the Lady of Lourdes as its pure and powerful patroness. Truth was the shining garment of Bernadette. The earth has caught and held its reflected glory.

I believe she brought the world close to Christ the Saviour because she set the example of saying short and simple prayers, representing universal yearning and universal need, yet suited to the limitations of the humble, the harassed and the weary. It was not in vain that she prayed in her pastureland, or held her rosary between relaxed fingers. She made us see, more clearly than many of us ever saw before, that we, too, may have the habit and the privilege of prayer whatever the conditions which surround our lives may be. There is always time to pray and always a place to pray. When we come to the consciousness of this, we cannot be far from the Throne of Divine Grace.

And finally, as I have said before, I believe she brought us close to Christ the Saviour because she herself first knew Him intimately as the Good Shepherd and therefore could reveal Him to the world as such: compassionate, long-suffering, mindful of the very least of His flock, tender with the weak, forgiving toward the errant, merciful to all. Such a figure does not seem distant or unreal: it seems near and true. No one is afraid to come to this Christ. We do so gladly and thankfully, and once in His presence our eyes are unsealed: we know that the Good Shepherd and the Divine Saviour are one.

The sublime shepherdess has shown us the way to find Him and to know Him.

144

⚙ REFERENCES ⚙

(1) This house, which is now occupied by a grand-daughter of Marie Avarant, has had its roof raised and now boasts two stories, but all the cooking is still done there over an open fire.

(2) This church was already in a state of dilapidation in 1844 and has since been demolished. It stood very near the Hospice de Lourdes, and its site is now marked by an impressive statue of Bernadette. A new parish church has been built a few blocks away. The record of Bernadette's baptism may still be seen at the *Mairie*.

(3) P. Lemaitre, *St. Bernadette*, p. 6.

(4) Pilgrimage to Notre Dame de la Salette, Diocese of Grenoble, owes its origin to the apparition of the Virgin, September 19, 1846, to Maximin Giraud, and Mélanie Mathieu. Devotion to Notre Dame de la Salette was authorized by Bishop Brouillard, May 1, 1852.

(5) The version used is that given by J. B. Estrade, who heard it over and over again from Bernadette's own lips.

(6) February 11, 1858. First apparition.

(7) According to Mère Marie Alphonse, who was the Superior of the Hospital Bernadette when I was her guest

in 1938, this observation was soon regarded as extremely significant and aroused the first suspicions regarding the identity of the Beautiful Lady. The *Pater Noster* and the *Ave* would logically be omitted by one who had no need to pray for her daily bread and would not therefore want to say part of the prayer and omit an important petition, while on the other hand she would gladly glorify the Trinity.

(8) February 14, 1858. Second apparition.

(9) February 18, 1858. Third apparition.

(10) The fourth apparition took place on February 19; the fifth, on February 20, 1858.

(11) Dr. Dozous went to the grotto for the first time on February 21, 1858, the occasion of the sixth apparition.

(12) There was another occasion later—March 3, 1858 —when Bernadette went to the grotto and the vision did not appear.

(13) February 23, 1858. Seventh apparition.

(14) February 20, 1858. Fifth apparition.

(15) P. Lemaitre, *St. Bernadette*, p. 13.

(16) February 24, 1858. Eighth apparition.

(17) February 21, 1858. Sixth apparition.

(18) February 26, 1858. Tenth apparition.

(19) February 25, 1858. Ninth apparition.

(20) February 27, 1858. Eleventh apparition.

(21) March 2, 1858. Fourteenth apparition.

(22) P. Lemaitre, *St. Bernadette*, p. 18.

(23) April 7, 1858. This was the seventeenth apparition.

(24) P. Lemaitre, *St. Bernadette*, p. 24.

(25) *Revue Bernadette*, June 1938, p. 154.

(26) This is the generally accepted version of the first

interview. Père Lemaitre, the Canon of the Motherhouse, however, points out that postulants are not permitted in the kitchen, and questions its authenticity. The contemporary annals of the Motherhouse reveal great rejoicing over Bernadette's arrival. But, after all, there is nothing contradictory between these entries and the prevailing conviction that she was coolly received, since all authorities admit that whatever the *feelings* of the Superior and the Mistress of Novices, they had agreed that Bernadette must be *treated* in a way that would increase her humility.

(27) *Revue Bernadette,* February 1939, p. 91.

(28) *Revue Bernadette,* June 1938, p. 169.

(29) *Revue Bernadette,* July 1938, p. 169.

(30) Charles Foing, *L'épanouissement d'une Ame aux Radieuses Leçons de la Vierge,* p. 139.

(31) This lacework now hangs in the parlor of the Bernadette Orphanage at Lourdes.

(32) The widow of Pierre Bernard Soubirous, Bernadette's youngest brother, was still living in Lourdes when I first went there. She had a remarkably gentle and lovely manner and a voice so soft and sweet that it is unforgettable for these qualities. Several of Bernadette's grand nephews and nieces are even yet living at Lourdes, where they are highly valued and respected members of society. Most of them are merchants or engaged in the hotel business.

(33) This sister and brother-in-law came to see her shortly before she died.

(34) In addition to this particular notebook, Bernadette also left several others similar to it, three copybooks filled with notes, and some loose leaves covered with them. All these writings reveal not only her exquisite pen-

148

manship and her clarity of thought, but also her spiritual vision.

(34-a) She has now died as have all the other nuns who knew her in the flesh.

(35) "Here rests in the peace of the Lord, Bernadette Soubirous, honored at Lourdes, in 1858, with many apparitions of the Blessed Virgin; in religion, Sister Marie Bernard, who died at Nevers at the Motherhouse of the Sisters of Charity on April 16, 1879, in the thirty-sixth year of her age and the twelfth of her religious profession."

(36) August 13, 1913.

(36-a) In this connection, it is interesting to see what Viola Sackville-West, a non-Catholic, has said about "the unaccountable problem of the incorruptibility of the body" in her scholarly work *The Eagle and the Dove,* where she compares, with meticulous thoroughness, the attributes of the two St. Theresas: "It is established beyond all doubt that the remains of certain persons, even after the lapse of centuries, have not suffered the ordinary decomposition of mortal flesh. On this point there can be no argument at all. Nor do the conditions following upon death and burial appear to affect the matter; it is influenced neither by damp, nor quicklime, nor by delay in interment. . . . From the moment we begin to glance, however cursorily, at this subject, the more baffling does it become. For one thing, the marvel of incorruptibility is extremely erratic in its incidence, and would seem not necessarily to be associated with the degree of sanctity. Thus, neither St. Francis, St. Bernard, St. Dominic . . . nor St. Thérèse of Lisieux, was spared the common lot of decay. On the other hand, this remarkable favour attends

149

some of the most famous names in the Calendar, St. Charles Borromeo for example, dying in 1584, was found almost entire in 1880 despite a damp and leaky coffin. . . . As for St. Teresa of Avila, we shall presently have occasion to record contemporary evidence on her preservation; and, coming down to more recent times, may note the case of the renowned Curé D'Ars, Jean-Baptiste Vianney, and *that of St. Bernadette Soubirous of Lourdes, who, dying in 1879, was exhumed thirty years later and found to be without any trace of putrefaction.*" (The italics are mine.)

(37) Near the end of her life, it will be recalled, Sister Marie Bernard had a tumor on her right knee.

(38) It will be recalled, from Sister Marie Marguerite's story, that this title had been conferred on Sister Marie Bernard six years earlier.

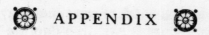# APPENDIX

BIBLIOGRAPHY—*French*

Bernadette la Petite Fille de Lourdes—Published by the Motherhouse of the Sisters of Charity of Nevers.

La Congrégation des Sœurs de Nevers—François Veuillot.

L'épanouissement d'une Ame aux Radieuses Leçons de la Vierge—Charles Foing.

Histoire Exacte de la Vie Intérieure et Religieuse de Ste. Bernadette—The Rev. H. Petitot, O.P. (This beautifully written book is considered by many of the authorities closest to the Motherhouse in Nevers to be somewhat prejudiced and opinonated. In this respect its standing is similar to that of Henri Ghéon's biography, *St. Thérèse de Lisieux*. Nevertheless, Petitot's thesis should be included in any bibliography of Bernadette for the same reason that Ghéon's biography should be included in any bibliography of Thérèse: its style and the standing of its author give it great distinction.)

Marie Révèle Jésus à Bernadette—Les XVIII Appels—D. Eugene Vandeur, O.S.B.

La Merveilleuse Histoire de Sainte Bernadette Soubirous —Jean de La Hire.

Quelque Membres de la Famille Soubirous—Pierre de Beauchamp.

Rayonnement Virginal—Published by the Motherhouse of the Sisters of Charity of Nevers.

Revue Bernadette—October 1932 through August 1939.

Sainte Bernadette—Canon E. Guynot, Superior of the Grand Seminary of Nevers.

Sainte Bernadette—Canon Lemaitre, Chaplain of Saint-Gildard.

Sainte Bernadette—Sœur Marie Bernard de la Congrégation des Sœurs de la Charité et de l'Instruction Chrétienne de Nevers—Mère Marie Thérèse Bordenave.

La Vie et l'Apotheose de Sainte Bernadette—Published by the Motherhouse of the Sisters of Charity of Nevers.

BIBLIOGRAPHY—*English*

The Appearances of the Blessed Virgin Mary at the Grotto of Lourdes—Personal Souvenirs of an Eyewitness—J. B. Estrade, translated from the French by J. H. le Breton Girdlestone, M.A., Oxon.

Bernadette of Lourdes—Margaret Gray Blanton, Longmans, Green and Company.